Contents

Theme 5   **Home Sweet Home**
Week 1 1
Reading-Writing Workshop:
    Personal Narrative 17
Week 2 19
Week 3 33
Taking Tests 49
Spelling Review 51

Theme 6   **Animal Adventures**
Week 1 53
Reading-Writing Workshop:
    Description 70
Week 2 72
Week 3 86
Taking Tests 99
Spelling Review 101

Theme 7   **We Can Work It Out**
Week 1 103
Reading-Writing Workshop:
    Story 117
Week 2 119
Week 3 132
Taking Tests 147
Spelling Review 149

Theme 8   **Our Earth**
Week 1 151
Reading-Writing Workshop:
    Research Report 164
Week 2 166
Week 3 180
Taking Tests 191
Spelling Review 193

Contents

Theme 9 Special Friends
Week 1 195
Reading-Writing Workshop:
  Friendly Letter 207
Week 2 209
Week 3 221
Taking Tests 234
Spelling Review 236

Theme 10 We Can Do It!
Week 1 238
Reading-Writing Workshop:
  Instructions 253
Week 2 255
Week 3 269
Taking Tests 281
Spelling Review 283

My Handbook 285
  Alphafriends 288
  Phonics/Decoding Strategy 290
  Reading Strategies 291
  Writing the Alphabet 292
  Spelling 300
    How to Study a Word
    Special Words for Writing
    Take-Home Word Lists
  Proofreading Checklist 327
  Proofreading Marks 327

Punchouts

Name _____

Week 1
Phonics Digraphs *sh, th, wh*

Words with *sh*, *th*, or *wh*

Circle the word that makes sense in the sentence. Write the word.

1. _____ are your friends?

   When   Who

2. Is _____ your pet bird?

   that   then

3. See the _____ !

   ship   shut

4. Is _____ your paper?

   them   this

Theme 5: **Home Sweet Home**   1

Week 1

Phonics Digraphs *sh, th, wh*

Name _____

Words with *sh*, *th*, or *wh*

Circle the word that names the picture.
Write the word.

1.  ship / fish

   _____

2.  path / math

   _____

3. 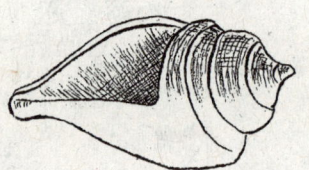 shed / shell

   _____

4. 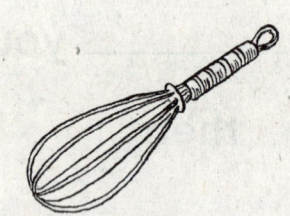 whisk / which

   _____

5. 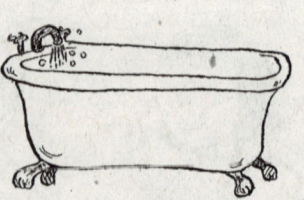 bath / with

   _____

6. 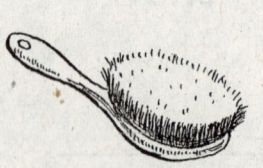 dish / brush

   _____

Theme 5: **Home Sweet Home**

Name _____

Words with ch or tch

Read the story. Write each **ch** or **tch** word in dark print below the picture it names.

Look at Jan **pitch**.
Mitch can **catch**.
Rich fell on a **branch**.
His **chin** got a scratch.

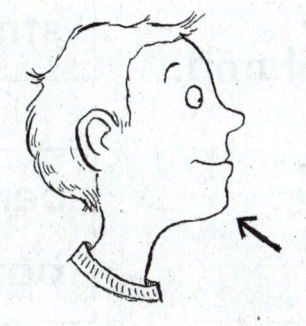

1. _____

2. _____

3. _____

4. _____

Week 1

Phonics Digraphs *ch, tch*

Name _____

Words with *ch* or *tch*

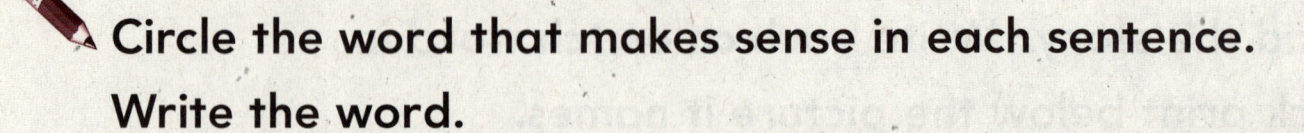

Circle the word that makes sense in each sentence. Write the word.

1. Let's eat _____ .

   | latch |
   | lunch |

2. I can _____ on the lamp.

   | switch |
   | stitch |

3. You can sit on the _____ .

   | bench |
   | batch |

4. Did you _____ this fish?

   | cast |
   | catch |

5. I got a big _____ !

   | bunch |
   | much |

4   Theme 5: **Home Sweet Home**

Name _____

Week 1
High-Frequency Words

Words to Know

Write a word from the box to complete each sentence.

1. My hat is too _____ .

2. I need more _____ in my hat!

3. These hats are too _____ .

4. When I _____ more, these hats will fit.

5. That hat is too _____ .

6. This other hat is just _____ .

| small |
| smell |

| room |
| these |

| more |
| long |

| grow |
| grass |

| other |
| light |

| right |
| room |

Theme 5: **Home Sweet Home** 5

Name _____

Words to Know

Week 1
High-Frequency Words

Read each pair of sentences. Draw a picture to go with them.

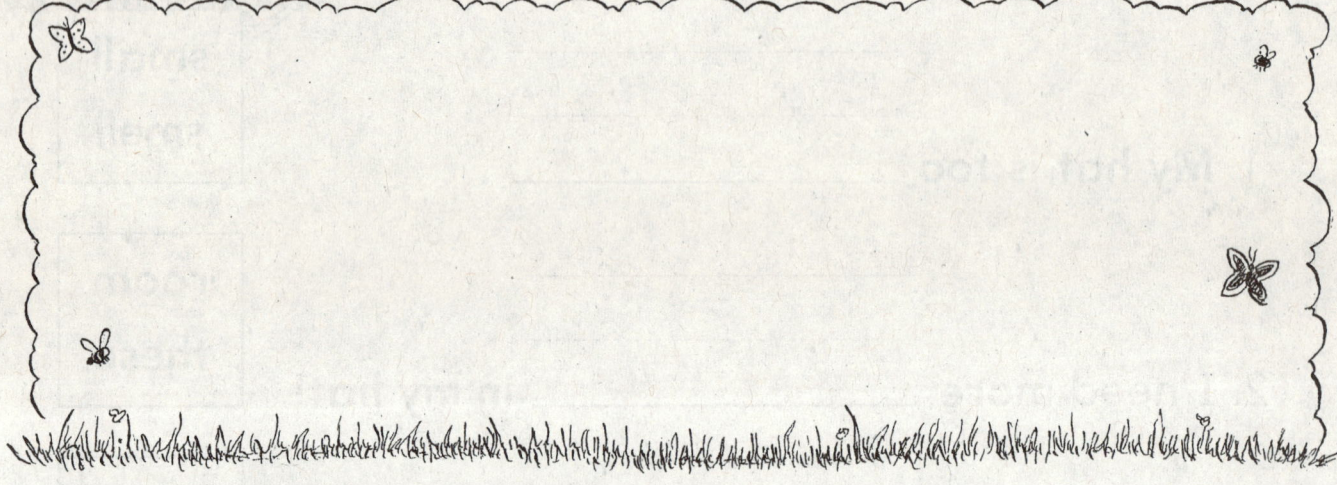

These flowers are small.
There is room to grow more!

Here is a long, light box.
This other box is just right.

6   Theme 5: **Home Sweet Home**

Name _____

Week 1

Story Vocabulary Moving Day

What's Inside?

Read the story. Draw a picture to show what happens.

What did Pam hide inside that plain box?
Is the box heavy?
Is it rough?
Wait! I see a hat inside.
It's a fancy hat!

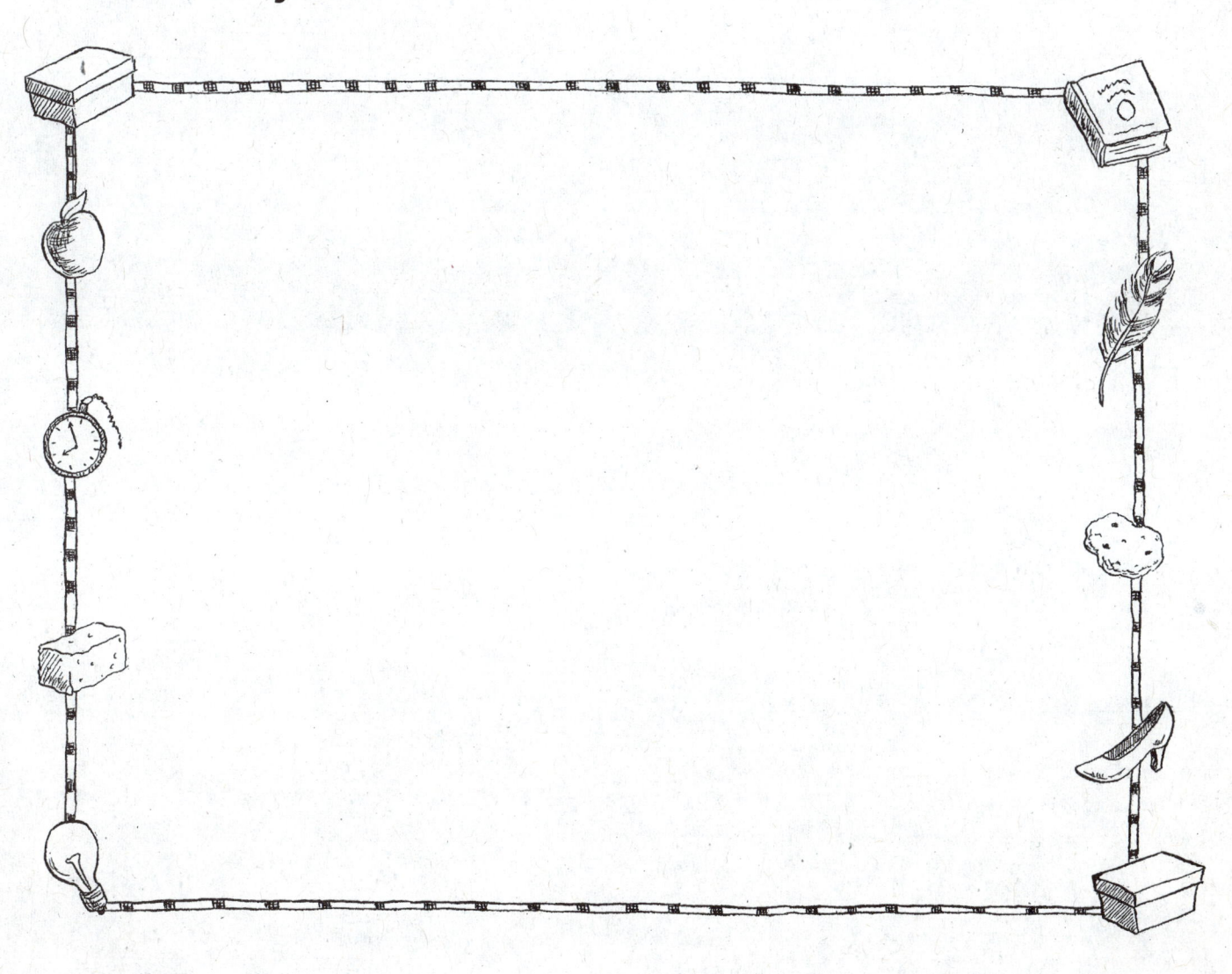

Theme 5: **Home Sweet Home** 7

Name _____

Week 1

Comprehension Check
Moving Day

Retell the Story!

Cut out and paste the sentences in order.
Read them to retell **Moving Day**.

1.
2.
3.
4.

| The next shells are too big and too small. | The crab finds a shell that is just right. |
| Many other shells will not do. | The crab's shell is snug. |

Theme 5: **Home Sweet Home**   9

Name _____

Week 1

Comprehension Compare and Contrast

Look at These Cars!

Read each set of sentences. Draw a picture to go with them.

This green car is big.
It is long.

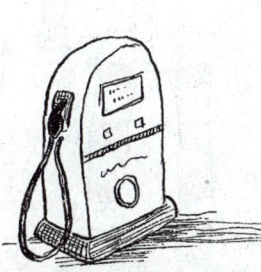 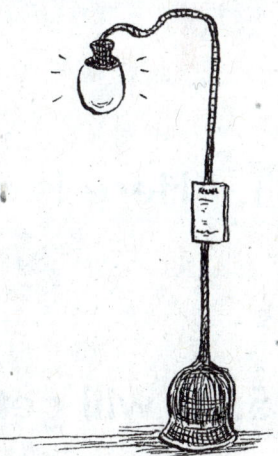

This brown car is small.
It is fancy.

Theme 5: **Home Sweet Home** 11

Name _____

Words Spelled with sh or ch

Week 1

Spelling Words Spelled with *sh* or *ch*

 Complete each sentence.

Word Bank

she
chin
fish
shell
much
chop

1. Jen did not have _____ lunch.

2. "I will go to the shop," _____ said.

3. Jen scratched her _____ .

4. "Here is a clam in its _____ ."

5. "I will get some _____ ."

6. Jen asked, "Can you _____ the fish?"

12 Theme 5: **Home Sweet Home**

Name _____

Opposites!

Week 1

Vocabulary Antonyms

Read each word. Circle its opposite in the box.

1. **first** | last   see   eat

2. **cold** | pass   hot   here

3. **go** | grow   run   stop

4. **down** | upon   here   up

5. **to** | from   do   four

6. **big** | light   small   right

7. **more** | big   long   less

8. **come** | go   catch   trip

Theme 5: **Home Sweet Home**   13

Name _____

Week 1

Grammar Exclamations

Exclamations

Read each pair of sentences. Circle the exclamation.

1. Look at these shells!

   Are these shells for Chip?

2. She can hold them.

   I want to hold them!

3. Can Mitch fetch them?

   He can do it!

4. Look at this bunch!

   I like the green batch.

5. What a long shell it is!

   The blue shell is small.

14   Theme 5: **Home Sweet Home**

Name _____

Spelling Spree

Write the missing letters to complete each Spelling Word. Write the word.

Spelling Words

| she | chin | fish | shell | much | chop |

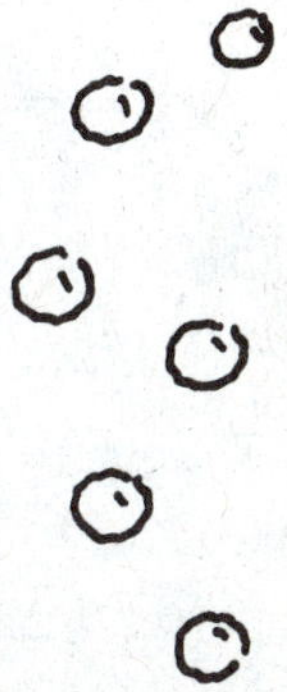

___ ___ op   ch ___ n   ___ ___ e

1. _____   2. _____   3. _____

Proofread each sentence. Circle each Spelling Word that is wrong, and write it correctly.

4. I will help you find a shill.

_____

5. That is too mutch for me to eat!

_____

6. I wish I had a pet fis.

_____

Theme 5: **Home Sweet Home** 15

Name _____

Week 1

Writing Writing Complete Sentences

My Sentences

 Look at each picture. Write a complete sentence about the picture.

1.

2.

16 Theme 5: **Home Sweet Home**

Name _____

Reading-Writing Workshop

Revising Your Personal Narrative

Revising Your Personal Narrative

✎ Put a check next to the sentences that tell about your personal narrative.

Superstar

☐ I used **I** in my story.
☐ I told what happened in a way that made sense.
☐ My story sounds like me talking.
☐ I told enough so the reader could tell what was going on in the story.
☐ My story has a good ending.
☐ I used complete sentences in my story.

Rising Star

☐ I did not use **I** in my story.
☐ Some of my story doesn't make sense.
☐ I need to add more so the reader can tell what is going on.
☐ My story needs a good ending.
☐ I need to fix some of the sentences in my story.

Theme 5: **Home Sweet Home** 17

Name _____

Reading-Writing Workshop

Improving Your Writing

Writing Sentences

Write each sentence correctly. Add a capital letter at the beginning. Add an end mark at the end.

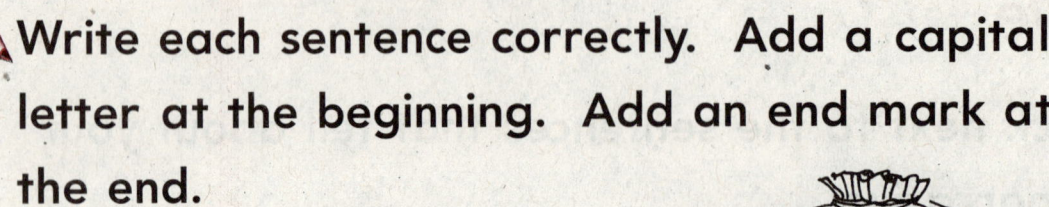

1. here is my hut

2. do you like my hut

3. cat likes it too

4. can you come in

18   Theme 5: **Home Sweet Home**

Week 2
Phonics Long a (CVCe)

Name _____

Long a

Circle the word that names each picture.
Write the word.

1.
gave
lace
gate

_____

2.
game
face
fake

_____

3.
cape
trace
cage

_____

4.
cage
cake
safe

_____

5.
skate
scale
lake

_____

6.
frame
rake
race

_____

Theme 5: **Home Sweet Home** 19

Week 2

Phonics Long *a* (CVC*e*)

Name _____

Long *a*

 Read the sentences. Write each word in dark print below the picture it names.

We swim in the **lake**.
We **skate** on the path.
Kate and I play a **game**.
We eat a **plate** of fish.

1.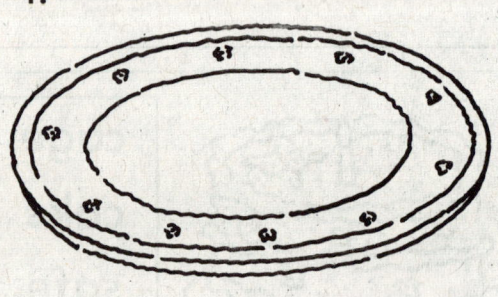
_____

2.
_____

3.
_____

4.
_____

20 Theme 5: **Home Sweet Home**

Name _____

Week 2
Phonics Final *nd, ng, nk*

Ends with nd, ng, or nk

Circle the word that makes sense in each sentence. Write the word.

1. The bird has hurt its _____ .
   sing   wing

2. It can't fly in the _____ .
   wind   bend

3. I _____ I can help.
   pink   think

4. It will take a _____ time.
   ring   long

5. But the bird will _____ .
   mend   lend

Theme 5: **Home Sweet Home**   21

Name _____

Words to Know

Circle the word that makes sense in each sentence. Write the word.

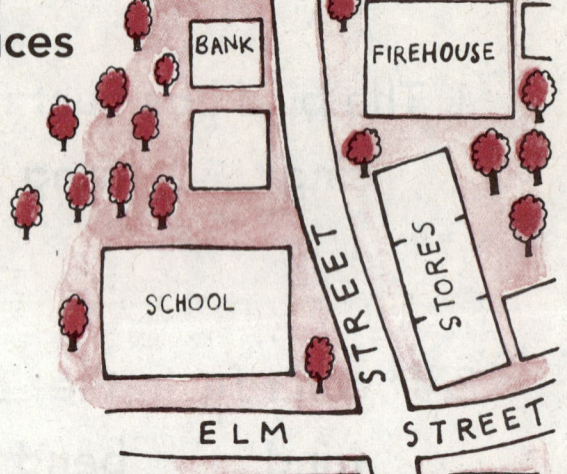

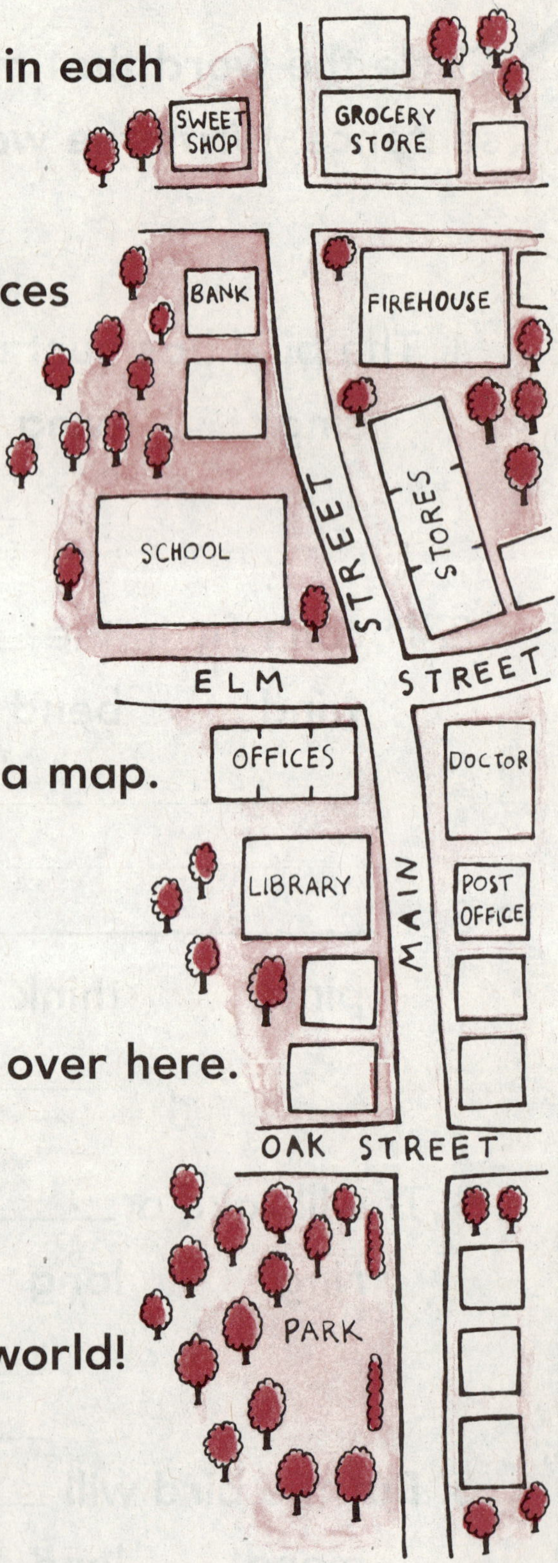

1. How could you see all the places
   _____
   in the _____ ?
   world   many

2. You _____ look at a map.
   cold   could

3. Your own _____ is over here.
   house   how

4. _____ take a look at the world!
   So   Some

Theme 5: **Home Sweet Home**

Week 2

High-Frequency Words

Name _____

Words to Know

Read the story, and do what it tells you to do.

    Dan said, "Could you make a world map? I have my own world map at my house. Would you like to come over and see it?"

Draw your own world map. Write sentences to tell how you did it.

Theme 5: **Home Sweet Home**   23

Name _____

Week 2

Story Vocabulary
Me on the Map

Story Words

Read the story. Use words from the box to complete the story.

Word Bank

ball   town   countries   Earth   giant

We live on _____. Earth looks

like a _____ green and blue

_____. All the people on Earth have

special places to live. These places are called

_____. In my country,

I live in a small _____ on a long street.

24   Theme 5: **Home Sweet Home**

Name _____

Week 2

Comprehension Check
Me on the Map

Put Them in Order!

✂ Cut and paste the pictures in order. Show how the girl found her special place on the map.

1. ☐   2. ☐   3. ☐

  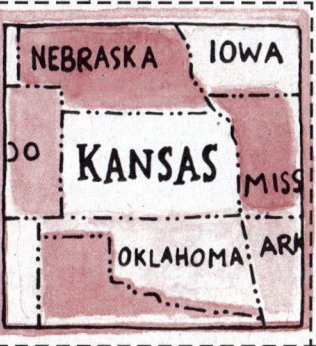

Theme 5: **Home Sweet Home** 25

Name _____

Week 2
Comprehension Making Generalizations

Why We Need Maps

Look at the pictures, and answer the questions below. Circle the answer.

Picture 1   Picture 2

1. In Picture 1, how do the people look?   sad   glad

2. In Picture 1, do they know where they are?   yes   no

3. How do the people look in Picture 2?   sad   glad

4. Did the people get help?   yes   no

Write a sentence to tell one thing maps can do.

_____
_____
_____
_____

Theme 5: **Home Sweet Home**   27

Name _____

Week 2

Spelling The Long *a* Sound

The Long *a* Sound

Word Bank

make   came   take   name   gave   game

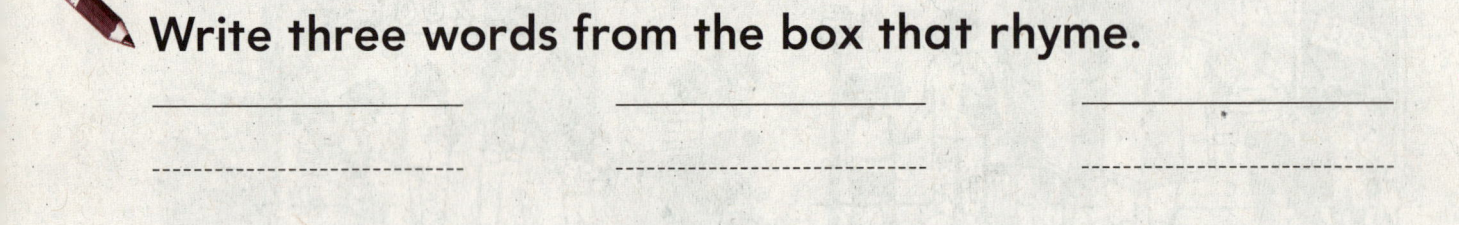

✏️ Write three words from the box that rhyme.

_____   _____   _____

28   Theme 5: **Home Sweet Home**

Name ______________________________

Week 2

Vocabulary Social Studies Words

All About Maps

Use the words from the box to label the picture.

Word Bank

map lake state

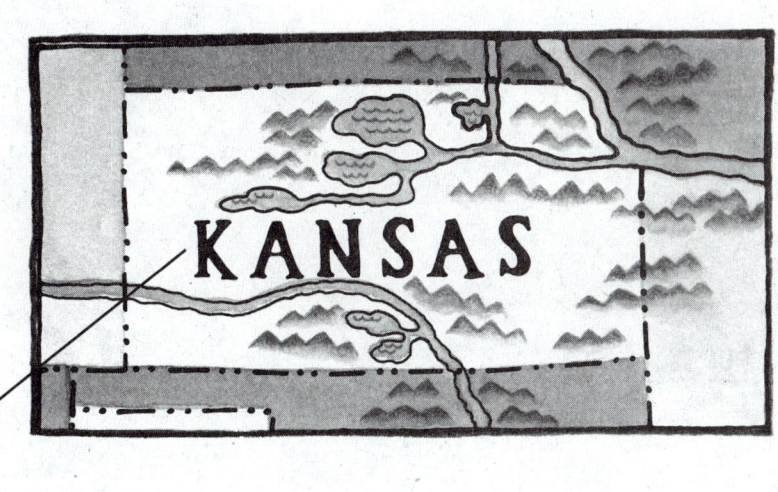

This is a ______________ of Kansas.

Name _____

Week 2

Grammar Which Kind of Sentence?

Which Kind of Sentence?

 Read each sentence. Write the correct mark at the end.

> . = tells you
> ? = asks you

1. Can I run in the race ___

2. That girl is fast ___

3. I can run fast, too ___

4. Who will win the race ___

5. Can I come in first ___

6. I win first place ___

30 Theme 5: **Home Sweet Home**

Name _____

Week 2
Spelling The Long *a* Sound

Spelling Spree

Write the missing letters to complete each Spelling Word. Write the word.

Spelling Words

make   came   take   name   gave   game

1. m ___ ___ e

2. t ___ k ___

3. g ___ m ___

4. c ___ m ___

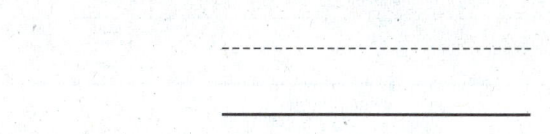

Proofread each sentence. Circle each Spelling Word that is wrong, and write it correctly.

5. My nam is Pat.

6. He gav that to me.

Theme 5: **Home Sweet Home**   31

Name _____

Week 2

Writing Writing a Journal Entry

A Day at School

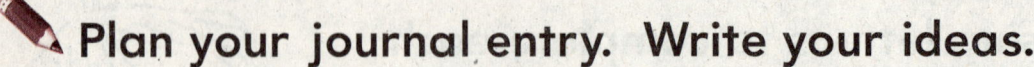 Plan your journal entry. Write your ideas.

Date: _____

What have you done at school today?

_____
_____
_____
_____
_____
_____
_____
_____

32 Theme 5: **Home Sweet Home**

Name _____

Week 3

Phonemic Awareness
Long *i* (CVC*e*)

Long *i*

Color the pictures whose names have the long **i** sound.

1.
2.
3.

4.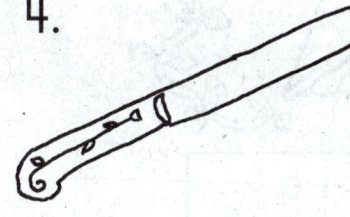
5.
6.

7.
8.
9.

Theme 5: **Home Sweet Home**   33

Name _____

Long *i*

Week 3

Phonics Long *i* (CVC*e*)

✏ Name each picture. Use the letters in the box to write the word.

e i p z r

1. __ __ __ __ __

n v i e

2. __ __ __ __

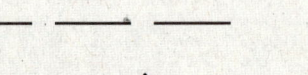

i m s e l

3. __ __ __ __ __

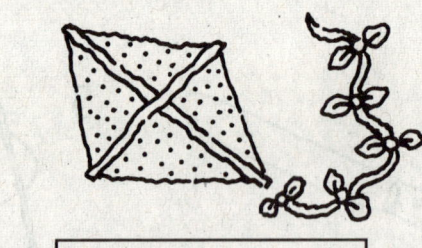

t k i e

4. __ __ __ __

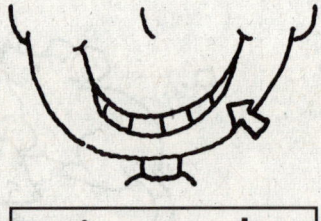

e b i k

5. __ __ __ __

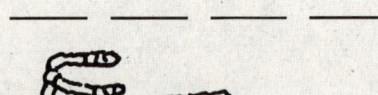

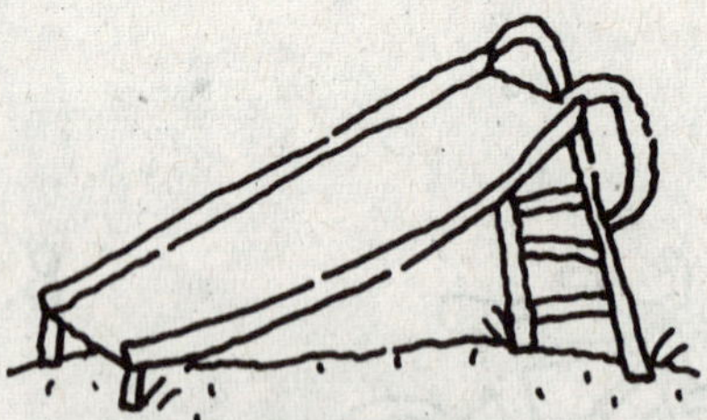

l d i s e

6. __ __ __ __ __

34 Theme 5: **Home Sweet Home**

Name _____

Week 3

Phonics Contractions

Contractions

Draw a line from each word pair to its contraction.

1. do not   isn't

2. is not   I'd

3. will not   we've

4. I would   it's

5. it is   won't

6. we have   don't

Write the word pair that makes up each contraction.

7. she'll

_____

_____

8. I'll

_____

_____

Theme 5: **Home Sweet Home** 35

Name _____

Words to Know

Write words from the box to complete the story.

Word Bank

give   our   good   little   fly

1. There was a _____ , strong wind.

2. Liz had a _____ kite.

3. Can we _____ her kite?

4. Let's _____ it a try.

5. We'll get _____ string.

Theme 5: **Home Sweet Home**

Name _____

Week 3

High-Frequency Words

Words to Know

Read each story. Draw a picture to show what happens.

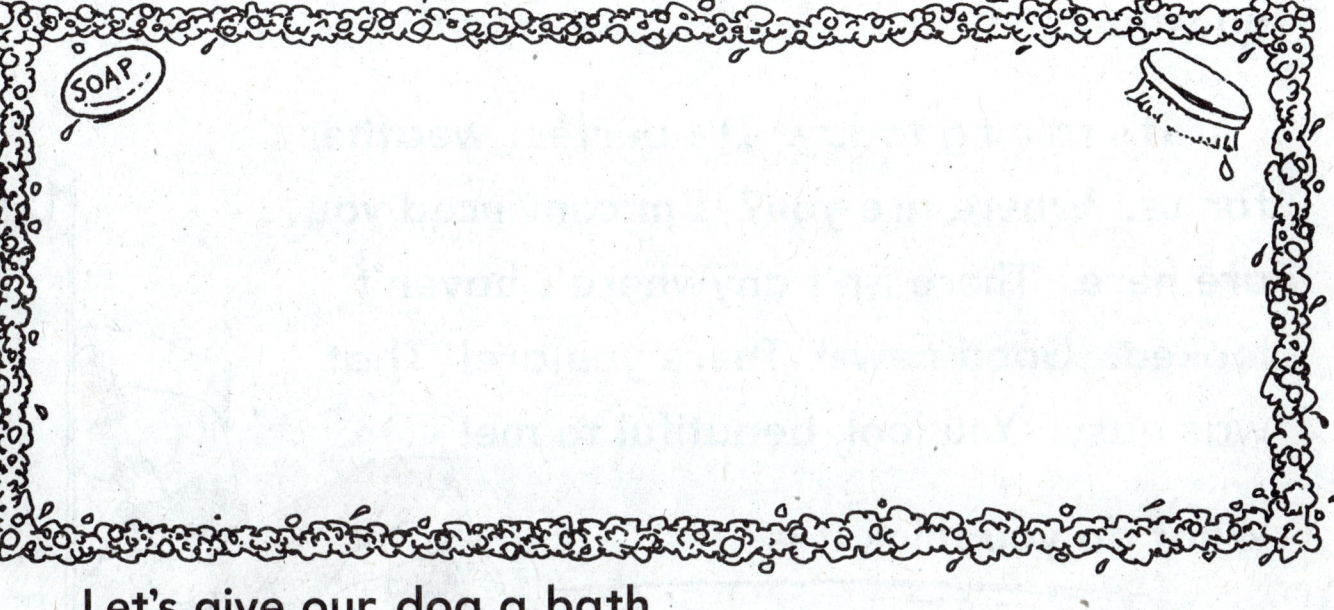

Let's give our dog a bath.
That was a good thing to do!

Her little bird can't fly yet.
She will try to help it.

Theme 5: **Home Sweet Home** 37

Name _____

Week 3

Story Vocabulary *The Kite*

Wet! Wet! Wet!

Read the clues. Draw a picture to answer the question.

It's raining today. It's perfect weather for us. Where are you? I'm convinced you are here. There isn't anywhere I haven't looked. Good news! There you are! That was easy! You look beautiful to me!

What do you think it is?

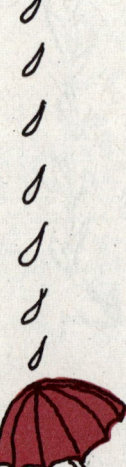

38   Theme 5: **Home Sweet Home**

Name _____

Week 3

Comprehension Check *The Kite*

What Happened?

Draw the beginning, middle, and end of **The Kite**. Write about the story.

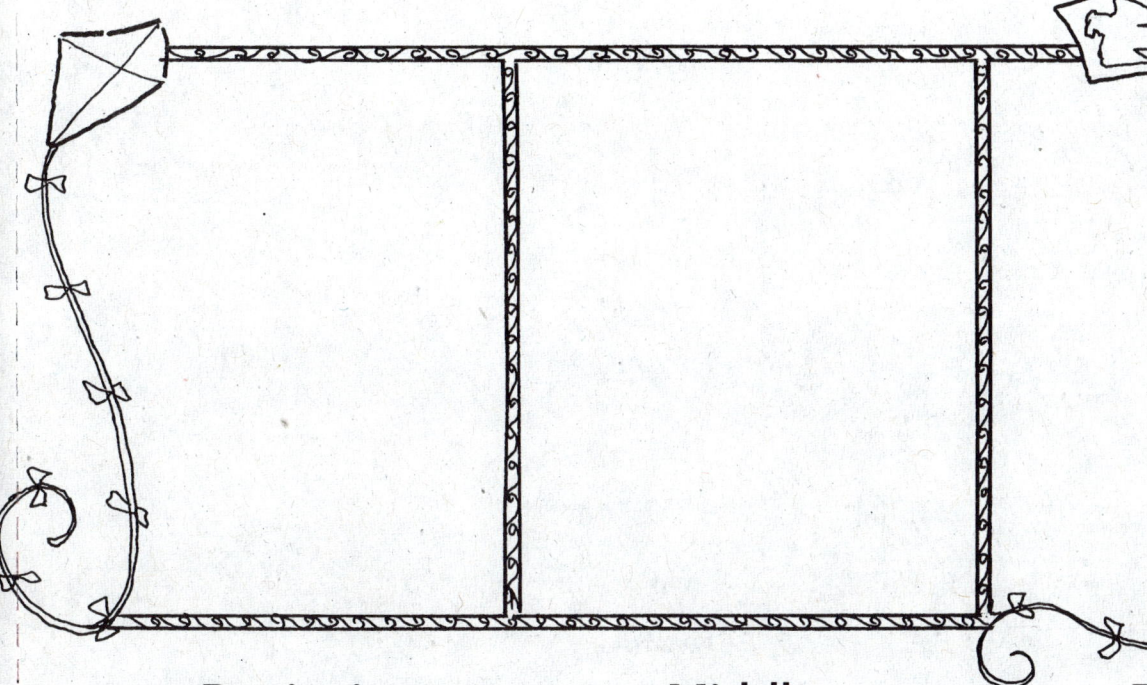

| Beginning | Middle | End |

Theme 5: **Home Sweet Home** 39

40

Name _____

Week 3

Comprehension Cause and Effect

What Happened?

Cut out and paste each effect next to its cause.

Cause
(Why it happens)

Effect
(What happens)

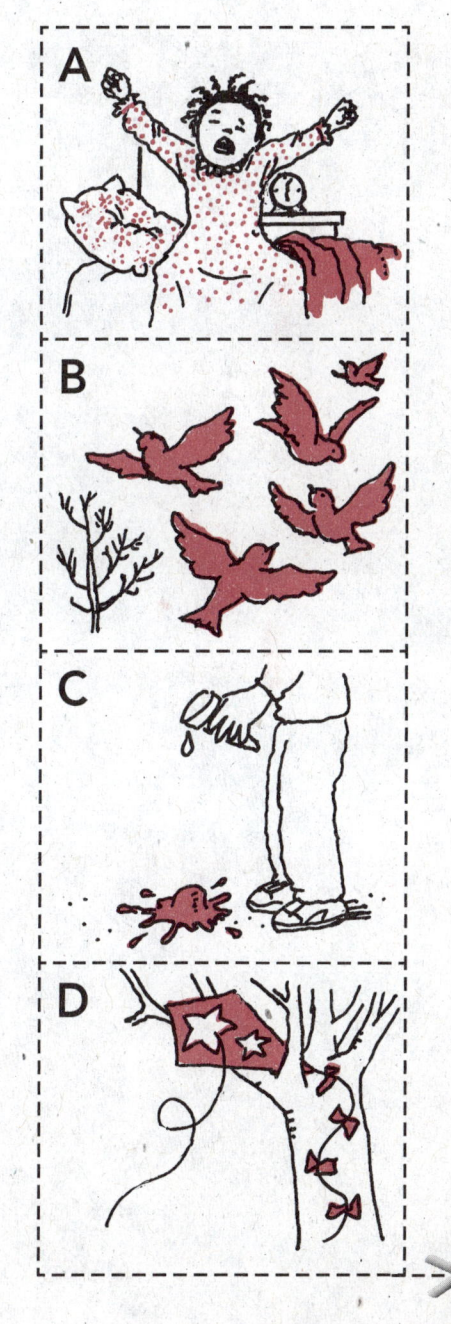

The cat runs.

The cone tips.

The bell rings.

The string snaps!

A

B

C

D

Theme 5: **Home Sweet Home**

42

Name _____

Week 3
Spelling The Long *i* Sound

The Long *i* Sound

Color the kites whose words have the long **i** sound.

Spelling Words

| like   five   ride   nine   time   kite |

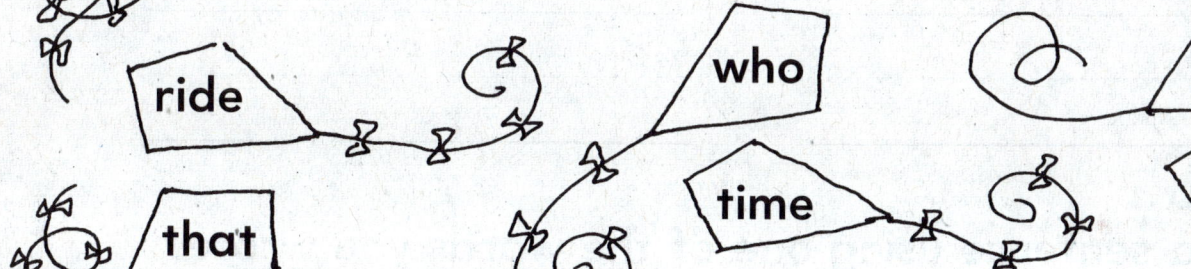

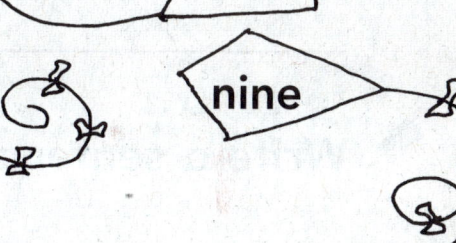

Kites shown with words: kid, like, ride, that, five, four, who, time, me, kite, you, nine

Write the Spelling Words from the kites you colored.

1. _____   2. _____   3. _____

4. _____   5. _____   6. _____

Theme 5: **Home Sweet Home**   43

Name _____

Week 3

Vocabulary Base Words with -ing

Words with -ing

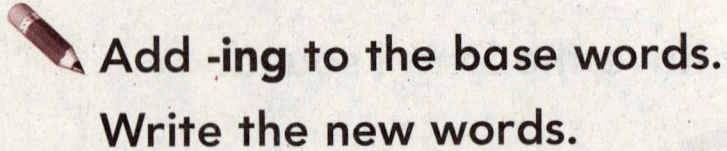

✏️ Add **-ing** to the base words. Write the new words.

-ing

walk

do

call

fly

✏️ Write a sentence using one of the words you wrote.

44 Theme 5: **Home Sweet Home**

Name _____

Week 3

Grammar Using *I* or *Me* in Sentences

Using *I* or *Me*

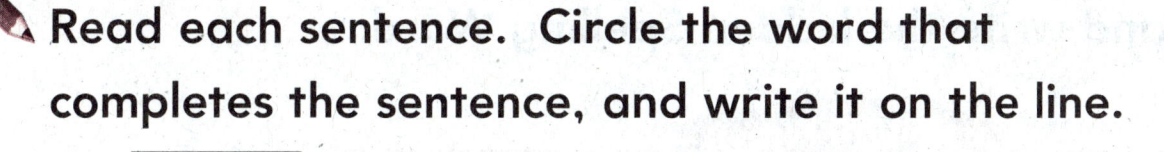

Read each sentence. Circle the word that completes the sentence, and write it on the line.

1. _____ have a big family.
       I   Me

2. Give _____ the can.
       me   I

3. My mother and _____ went to the lake.
       me   I

4. Can you come with _____ ?
       I   me

Write a sentence using **I** or **me**.

_____

_____

_____

Theme 5: **Home Sweet Home**   45

Week 3
Spelling The Long *i* Sound

Name _____

Spelling Spree

Circle and write the hidden Spelling Word.

Spelling Words

| like | five | ride | nine | time | kite |

1. eninep

2. timeur

3. cfiveg

Proofread each sentence. Circle each Spelling Word that is wrong, and write it correctly.

4. I like to rid my bike.

5. I like to fly my cit.

6. Do you lik these things, too?

46 Theme 5: **Home Sweet Home**

Name _____

Writing a Paragraph

Week 3
Writing Writing a Paragraph

✏ Write a sentence about an animal you like. This will be your main idea.

_____
_____
_____
_____

✏ Write two sentences telling why you like this animal.

_____
_____
_____
_____
_____
_____
_____
_____

Theme 5: **Home Sweet Home** 47

Name _____

Phonics

Home Sweet Home
Taking Tests

Now use what you have learned about taking tests. Your teacher will tell you what to do. This practice will help you when you take this kind of test.

1   grab   sack   ship   rush
         ○   ○   ○   ○

2   thin   shop   when   tell
         ○   ○   ○   ○

3   shop   cat   dish   chop
         ○   ○   ○   ○

Theme 5: **Home Sweet Home**   49

Name _____

Phonics continued

4   back   gave   kite   bug
    ○   ○   ○   ○

5   hill   name   like   hid
    ○   ○   ○   ○

6   take   pad   gap   side
    ○   ○   ○   ○

Home Sweet Home
Taking Tests

Home Sweet Home:
Theme 5 Wrap-Up

Spelling Review

Name _____

Spelling Review

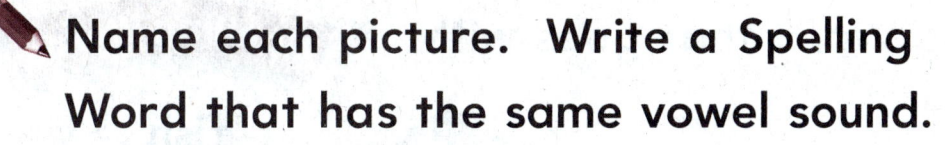

✏️ Name each picture. Write a Spelling Word that has the same vowel sound.

1. _____

2. _____

Spelling Words

shell
fish
chop
much
gave
kite

✏️ Write two Spelling Words that have **ch**.

3. _____

4. _____

✏️ Write two Spelling Words that have **sh**.

5. _____

6. _____

Theme 5: **Home Sweet Home** 51

Name _____

Home Sweet Home:
Theme 5 Wrap-Up
Spelling Review

Spelling Spree

Write the Spelling Word that goes with each picture.

Spelling Words

fish
chop
make
like
name
ride

1. I have on a _____ tag.

2. He will _____ it down.

3. The _____ can see a bug.

Proofread each sentence. Circle each Spelling Word that is wrong, and write it correctly.

_____

4. Let the kite ried on the wind.

_____

5. Mak the kite go up, up, up!

_____

6. It can fly lik a bird.

52   Theme 5: **Home Sweet Home**

Name _____

Week 1

Phonics Long *o*

Long o

Circle the word that goes with each picture, and write it on the line.

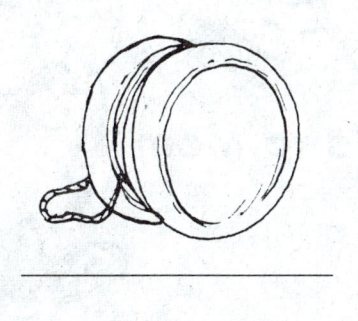

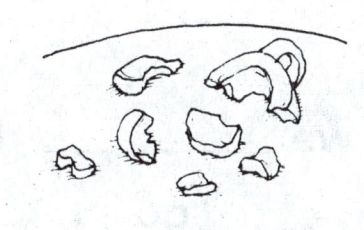

1. _____   yo-yo / fish / yam

2. _____   bake / broke / clock

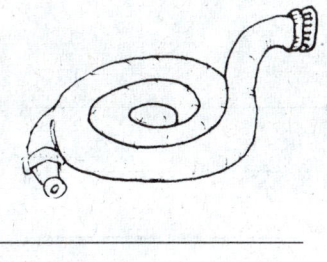

3. _____   hope / mug / hose

4. _____   cane / cone / drum

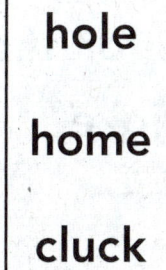

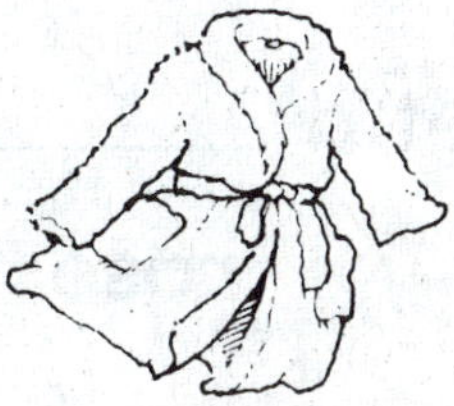

5. _____   hole / home / cluck

6. _____   rose / room / robe

Theme 6: **Animal Adventures**

Week 1

Phonics Long *o*

Name _____

Long *o*

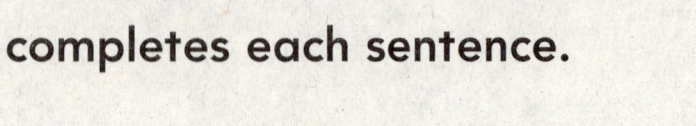

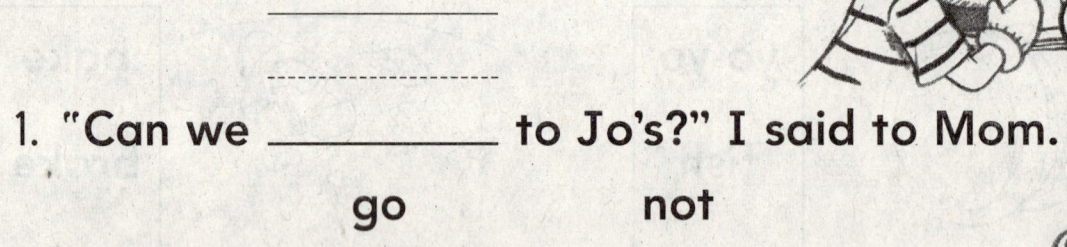

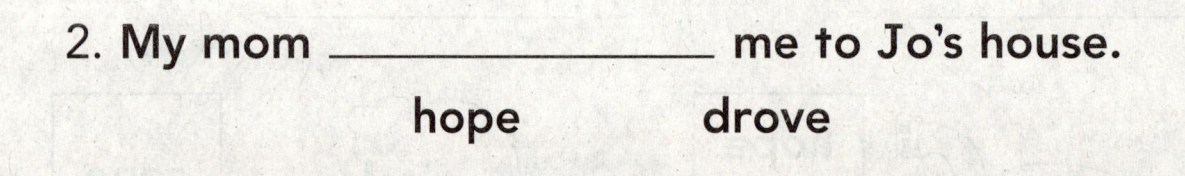

Circle and write the word that completes each sentence.

_____

1. "Can we _____ to Jo's?" I said to Mom.

    go   not

_____

2. My mom _____ me to Jo's house.

    hope   drove

_____

3. We can fix eggs on Jo's play _____.

    froze   stove

_____

4. "Let's get a _____ for that vase," I said.

    rose   joke

_____

5. We wet the grass with the _____.

    stone   hose

54   Theme 6: **Animal Adventures**

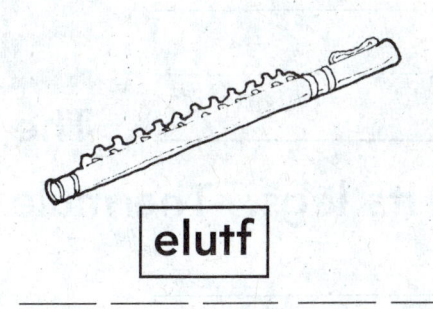

Name _____

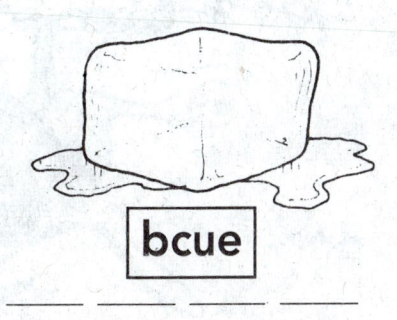

Week 1

Phonics Long *u*

Long *u*

Use the letters in the box to write the word that goes with each picture.

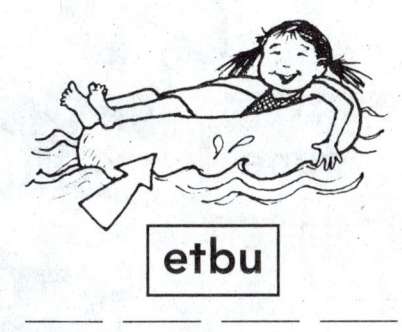

etbu	utec

1. _____ 2. _____

heug	elutf

3. _____ 4. _____

ulme	bcue

5. _____ 6. _____

Theme 6: **Animal Adventures** 55

Week 1

Phonics Long *u*

Name _____

Long *u*

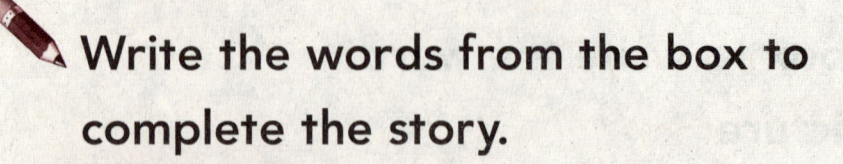

Write the words from the box to complete the story.

Word Bank

| flute | huge | cute | mule | tune |

The girl plays a _____ on the _____ . The _____ kicks its legs. The mule gives the girl a _____ kiss. It's so _____ !

56 Theme 6: **Animal Adventures**

Name _____

Week 1

Phonics Final *ft, lk, nt*

Ends with *ft*, *lk*, or *nt*

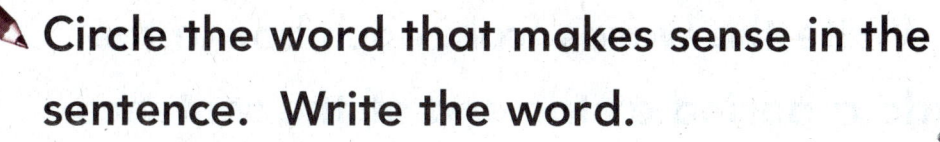

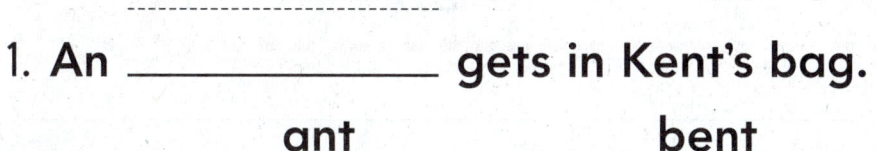

Circle the word that makes sense in the sentence. Write the word.

1. An _____ gets in Kent's bag.

   ant   bent

2. Kent and the ant have hot dogs and _____.

   sulk   milk

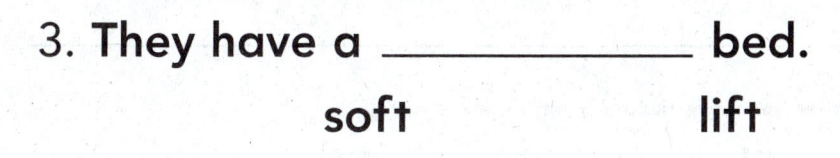

3. They have a _____ bed.

   soft   lift

4. Kent and the ant _____ the camp.

   gift   left

5. The ant _____ the trip with Kent!

   spent   cent

Theme 6: **Animal Adventures**   57

Name _____

Week 1
High-Frequency Words

Words to Know

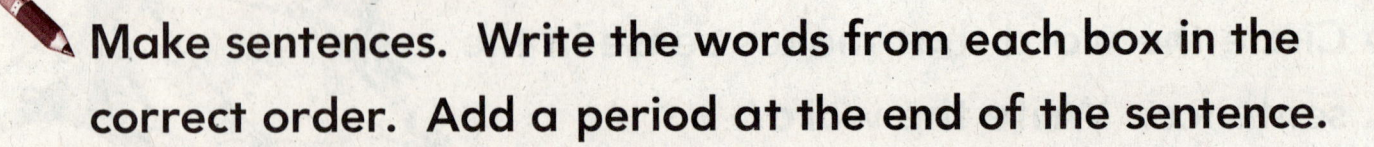

Make sentences. Write the words from each box in the correct order. Add a period at the end of the sentence.

    a bird one by I found morning house my

_____
_____

    shout my to I out dad

_____
_____

    how climb to nest Show the me to

_____
_____

58   Theme 6: **Animal Adventures**

Name _____

Words to Know

Week 1
High-Frequency Words

Read each pair of sentences. Circle the sentence that tells about the picture.

You do not have to shout!

I know that girl.

I will show you how to ride.

I ate too much!

In the morning, I climb out of bed fast.

Here is my mother.

My room is big.

I found a dime by the swing.

Theme 6: **Animal Adventures**   59

Name _____

Week 1

Story Vocabulary *The Sleeping Pig*

Story Vocabulary

Read the story. Use the box to help you find and circle some words from **The Sleeping Pig**.

Word Bank

began
celebrate
coyote
cricket
howl
rabbit
tail
watermelon

It was fall, so Cricket said, "Let's celebrate!" Coyote let out a howl. Rabbit jumped and twitched his tail up and down.

Then they began to eat a huge watermelon!

Draw a picture to go with the story.

60   Theme 6: **Animal Adventures**

Name _____

Week 1

Comprehension Check *The Sleeping Pig*

Who Tried to Wake Up Mrs. Pig?

Draw one animal that helped Celina.

Write about what that animal did.

_____
_____
_____
_____
_____
_____

Theme 6: **Animal Adventures** 61

Name _____

Week 1

Comprehension Story Structure

Problems, Problems

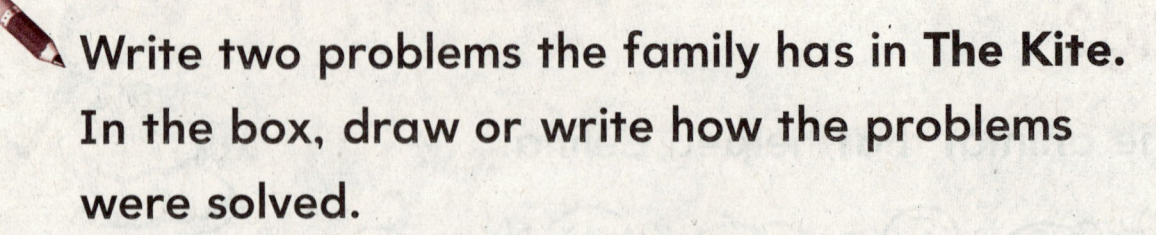

Write two problems the family has in **The Kite**. In the box, draw or write how the problems were solved.

Problems

_____
_____
_____
_____
_____
_____

Solutions

Theme 6: **Animal Adventures**

Name _____

The Long o Sound

Color the pigs whose words have the long o sound.

Spelling Words

go   bone   so   nose   home   no

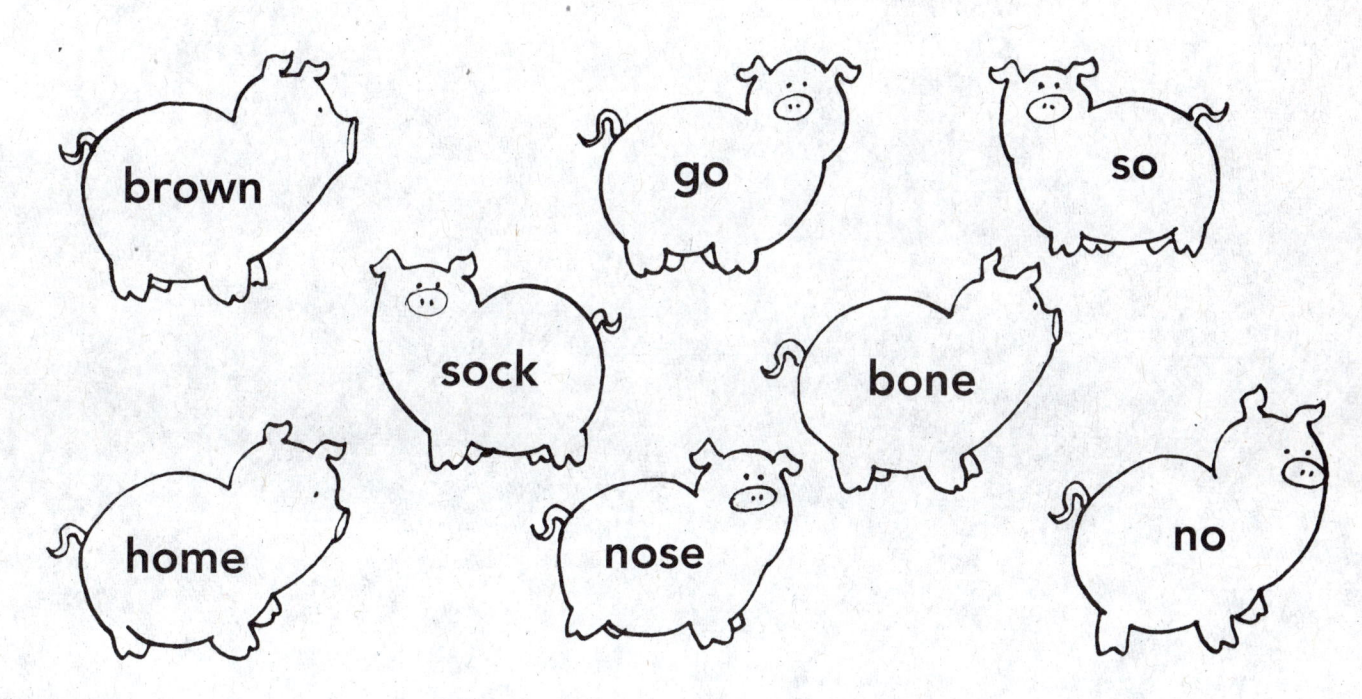

(pigs with words: brown, go, so, sock, bone, home, nose, no)

Write the Spelling Words from the pigs you colored.

1. _____   2. _____   3. _____

4. _____   5. _____   6. _____

Theme 6: **Animal Adventures**   63

Week 1

Vocabulary Alphabetical Order

Name _____

ABC Order

Cut out and paste the words in ABC order.

A B C D E F G H I J K L M N O P Q R S T U V W X Y Z

1.

2.

3.

4.

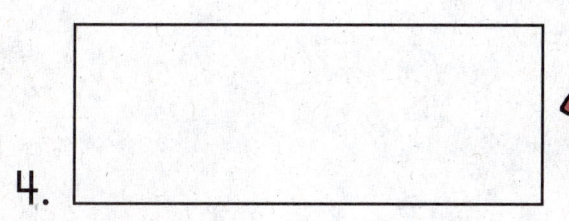

give

could

shout

fly

Theme 6: **Animal Adventures** 65

Name _____

Week 1

Grammar Naming Words for People and Animals

Naming Words

Help the pig find the watermelon patch. Draw a line to connect the naming words.

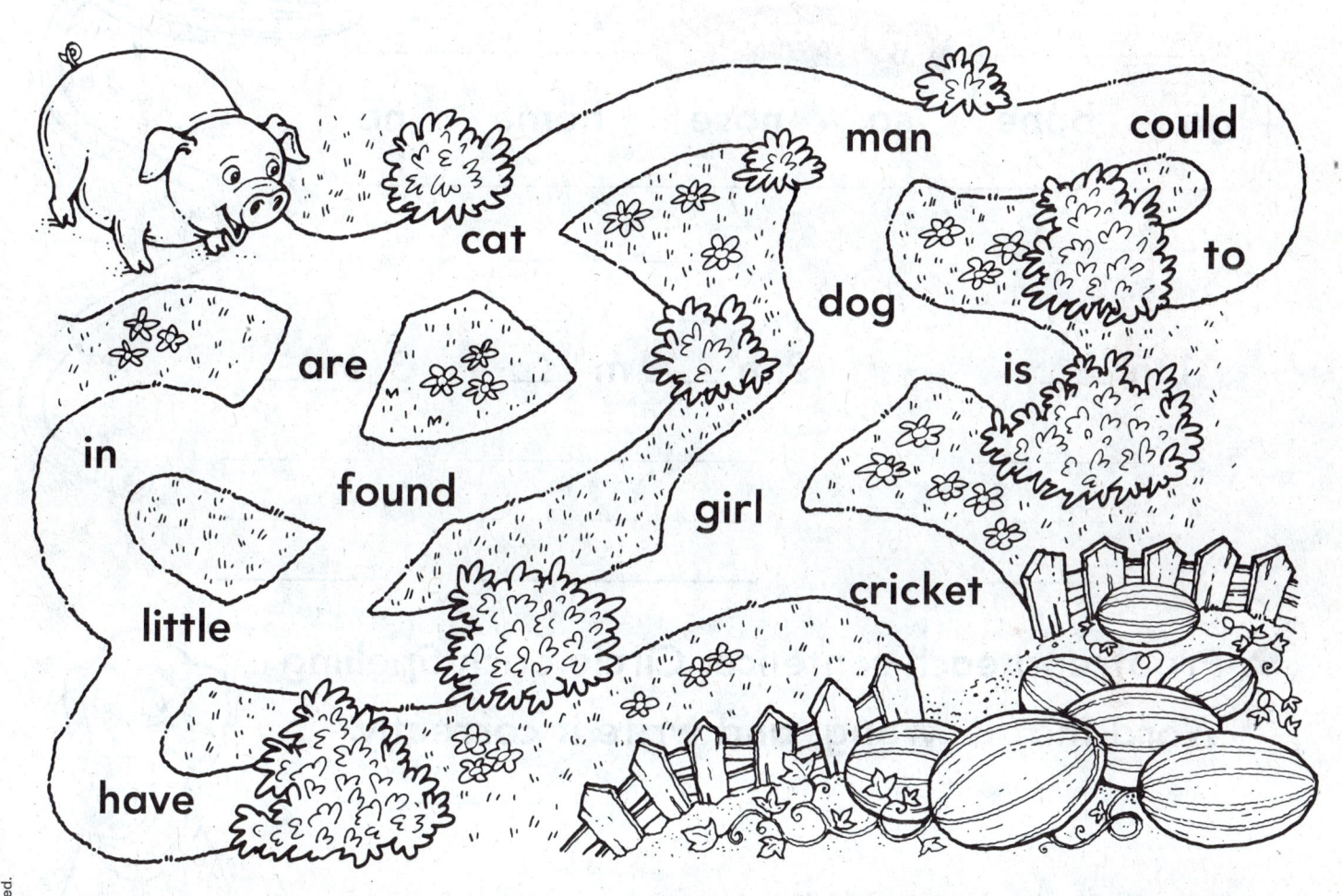

man could
cat to
dog
are is
in found
little girl
    cricket
have

Choose two naming words from above and write them below.

_____   _____

Theme 6: **Animal Adventures** 67

Week 1

Spelling The Long *o* Sound

Name _____

Spelling Spree

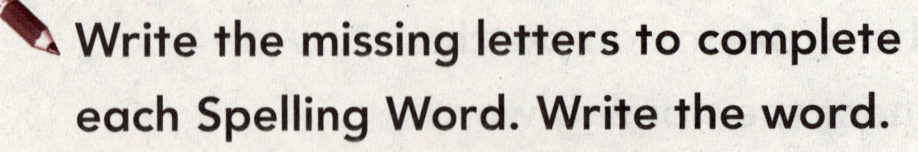

✏️ Write the missing letters to complete each Spelling Word. Write the word.

Spelling Words

| go | bone | so | nose | home | no |

1. n __

2. h __ m __

3. s __

✏️ Proofread each sentence. Circle each Spelling Word that is wrong, and write it correctly.

1. The dog hid the bon. _____

2. It got mud on its noze. _____

3. Goe get the hose! _____

68　Theme 6: **Animal Adventures**

Name _____

List Your Reasons

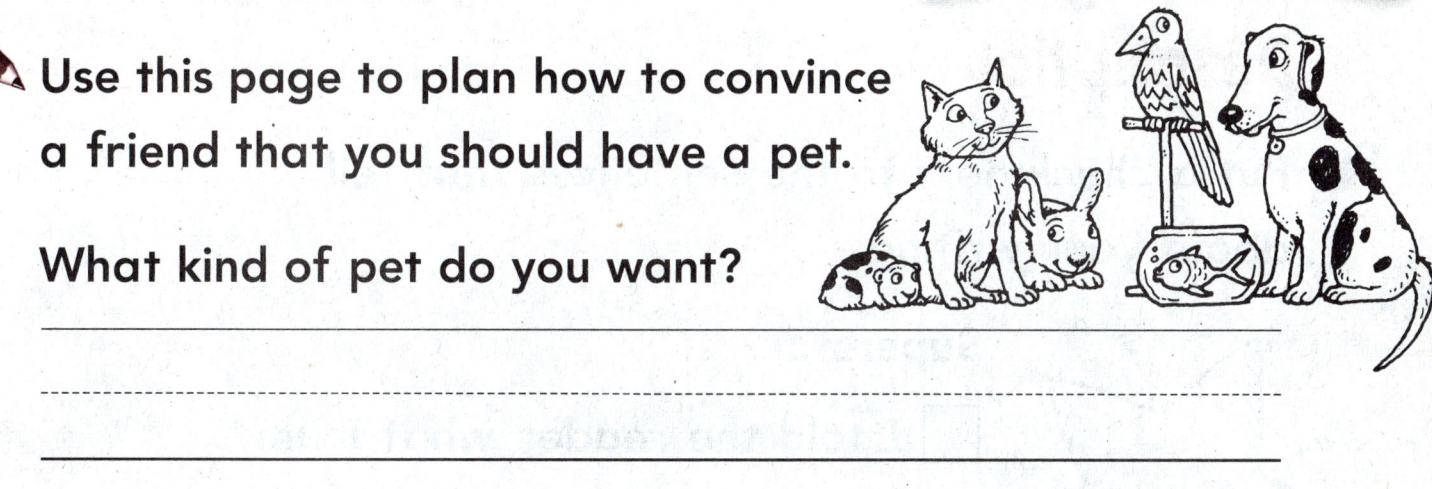

Use this page to plan how to convince a friend that you should have a pet.

What kind of pet do you want?
_____
_____

Write why you should get that pet.
_____
_____
_____
_____
_____
_____
_____

Read what you wrote to a friend. What can you add?
_____
_____
_____
_____

Name _____

Reading-Writing Workshop

Revising Your Description

Revising Your Description

✏️ Put a check next to the sentences that tell about your writing.

Superstar

☐ I told the reader what I am describing.

☐ My description tells how something looks, feels, sounds, tastes, and smells.

☐ My description uses exact words.

☐ My description makes a clear picture for the reader.

Rising Star

☐ I need to tell what I am describing.

☐ I need to add words that tell how something looks, feels, sounds, tastes, and smells.

☐ I could change some of my words to more exact words.

☐ I could make a clearer picture for the reader.

70 Theme 6: **Animal Adventures**

Name _____

Writing Sentences

Read each group of words. Cross out the one that is not a sentence. Copy the sentence on the line.

1. Paul and Gina.
   Paul and Gina ran to the gate.

2. The snake.
   The snake slid under the rock.

3. Kendra and I watched the bears.
   The bears.

4. The monkey climbed the tree.
   The top of the tree.

Name _____

Week 2

Phonics Long *e*

Long *e*

🖍 **Color each shape that has a long e word.**

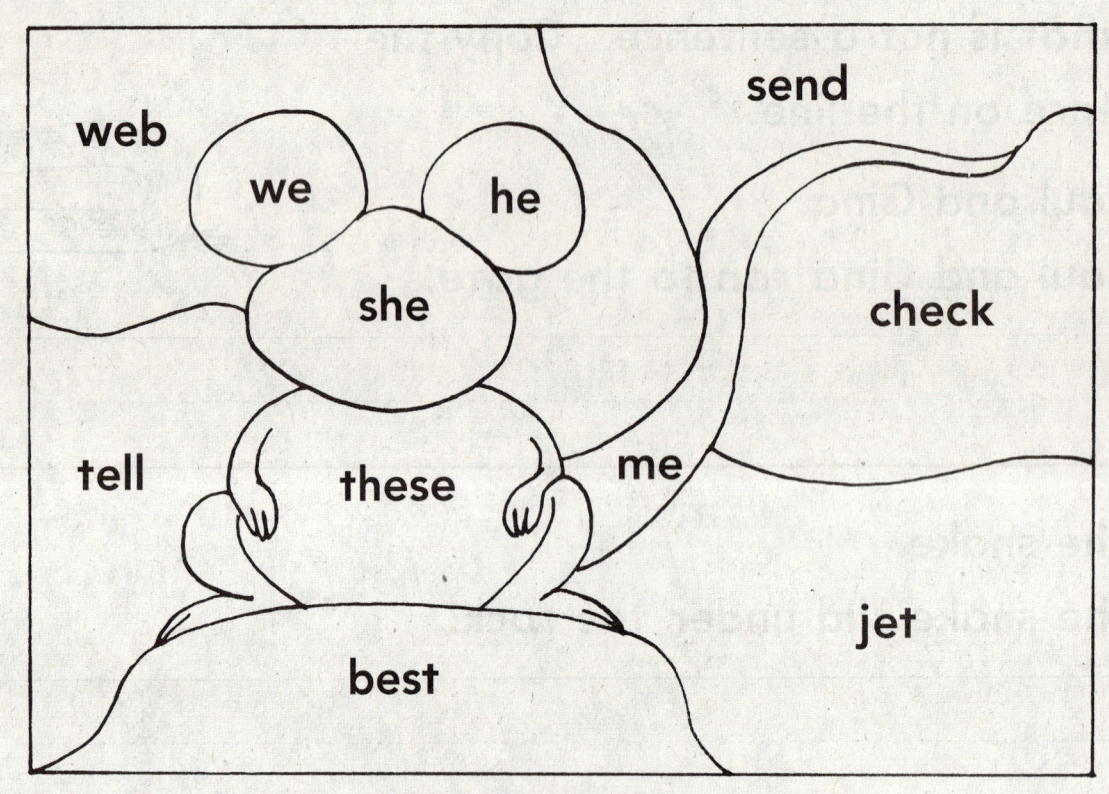

```
web          send
    we    he
       she            check
tell   these   me
         best       jet
```

✏️ **Write each of the words you colored.**

1. _____   2. _____

3. _____   4. _____

5. _____

72 Theme 6: **Animal Adventures**

Week 2

Phonics Long e

Name _____

Long e

Read the story. Circle all the words with the long e sound.

My friend Pete came to me with a plan. We can have a play. These friends can be in it — Steve, Rose, and Mel. The theme of our play can be "Friends."

Draw a picture to go along with the story.

Theme 6: **Animal Adventures**   73

Week 2

Phonics Vowel Pairs *ee, ea*

Name _____

Words with *ee, ea*

Read each word. If the word has long e spelled **ea**, write it under **peach**. If the word has long e spelled **ee**, write it under **jeep**.

Word Bank			
bean	sheep	seat	beep
keep	eat	teeth	beach

peach

1. _____

3. _____

5. _____

7. _____

jeep

2. _____

4. _____

6. _____

8. _____

74   Theme 6: **Animal Adventures**

Week 2

Phonics Vowel Pairs *ee, ea*

Name _____

Words with ee, ea

Read each sentence. Write each word in dark print below the picture it names.

A **bee** stung a dog.
The dog broke its **leash**.
The dog ran to a **tree**.
The dog ate a **peach**.

1. _____

2. _____

3. _____

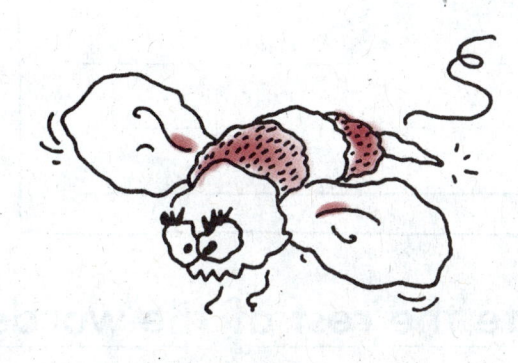

4. _____

Theme 6: **Animal Adventures** 75

Name _____

Week 2

High-Frequency Words

Words to Know

Write the words that name things in a house in the house shape. Write the words that name things that live in a barn in the barn shape.

Word Bank

| cow | table | now | door |
| there | through | horse | wall |

Write the rest of the words.

76 Theme 6: **Animal Adventures**

Name _____

Words to Know

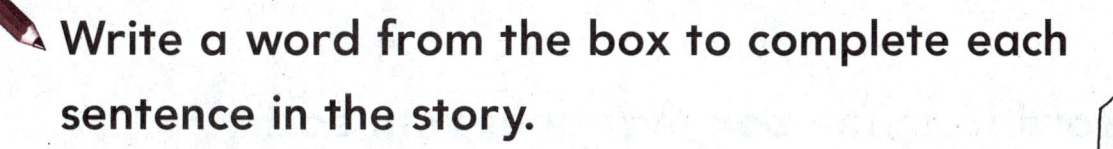

Week 2
High-Frequency Words

Write a word from the box to complete each sentence in the story.

Word Bank

table   there   horse   through   wall

1. The _____ walked through the door.

2. The cow walked _____ the door.

3. The horse sat at the _____ .

4. The cow sat by the _____ .

5. Now _____ was a funny picture!

Theme 6: **Animal Adventures**   77

Name _____

Week 2

Story Vocabulary EEK! There's a Mouse in the House

EEK! Look at These Words!

Write a word from the box that goes with each picture.

Word Bank

| marched | elephant | tangled |
| dancing | barn | mouse |

1. _____
2. _____
3. _____
4. _____   
5. _____
6. _____

Theme 6: **Animal Adventures**

Name _____

Week 2

Comprehension Check *EEK! There's a Mouse in the House*

What's It All About?

Read each sentence. Then draw a line from the sentence to the picture that completes it.

1. The cat knocked over a

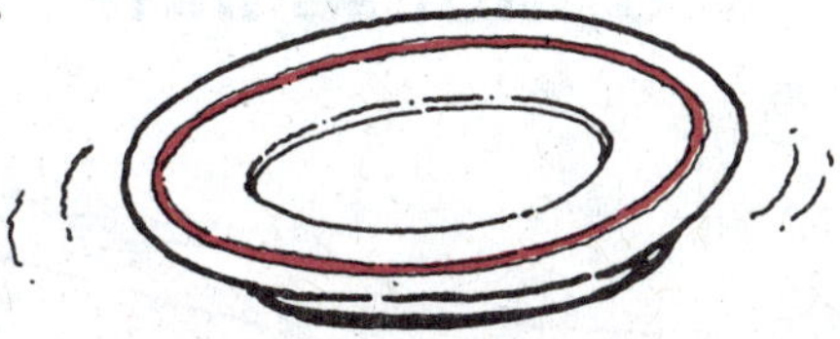

2. The dog broke a

3. The hog ate

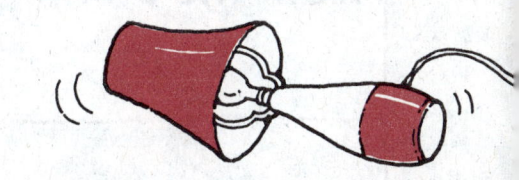

4. The sheep got tangled in

5. The hen was laying eggs on the

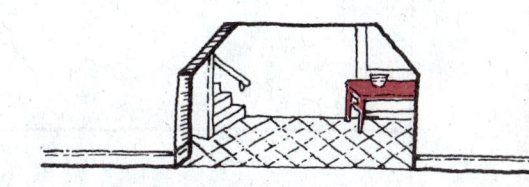

6. The elephant went in through the

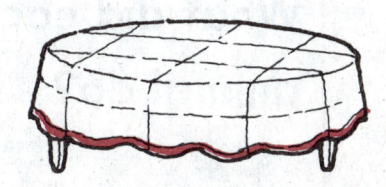

Theme 6: **Animal Adventures** 79

Name _____

Week 2

Comprehension Noting Details

Details from the Story

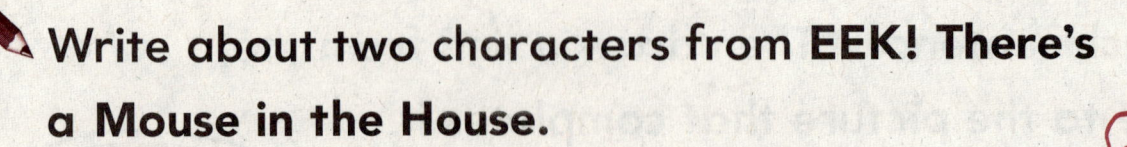

Write about two characters from **EEK! There's a Mouse in the House.**

Name two animals from the story.		
Did each animal help?		
What did each animal do?		

80 Theme 6: **Animal Adventures**

Name _____

The Long e Sound

Week 2

Spelling The Long e Sound

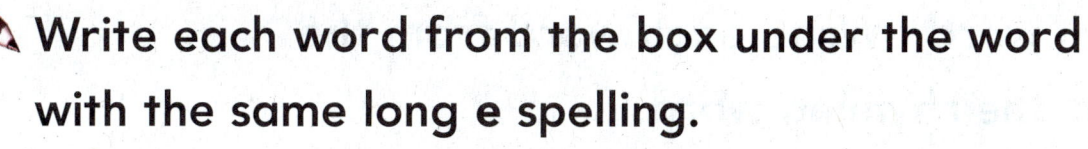

Write each word from the box under the word with the same long e spelling.

Spelling Words

| me | see | mean | feet | eat | he |

we   meet   treat

1. _____   2. _____   3. _____

4. _____   5. _____   6. _____

Draw a silly picture to match the silly sentence.

He sees mean beans that eat feet.

Theme 6: **Animal Adventures**   81

Week 2
Vocabulary Rhyming Words

Name _____

Rhyme Time!

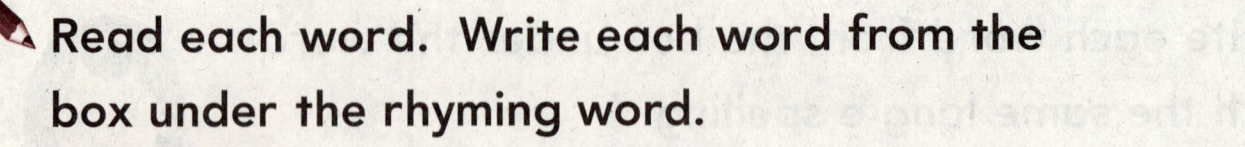

Read each word. Write each word from the box under the rhyming word.

Word Bank

mole	fake	three
we	hole	take
wake	me	role

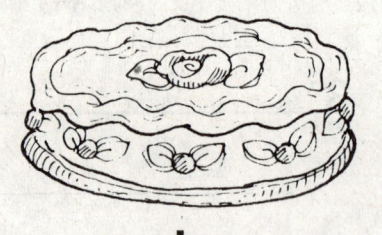

cake 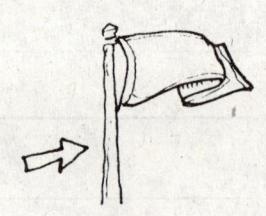   **pole**    **he**

Name _____

Week 2

Grammar Naming Words for Things and Places

Naming Words

Read each sentence. Circle the naming word and draw a picture of it.

1. Here is a green vase.

2. That house is small.

3. Where is my sled?

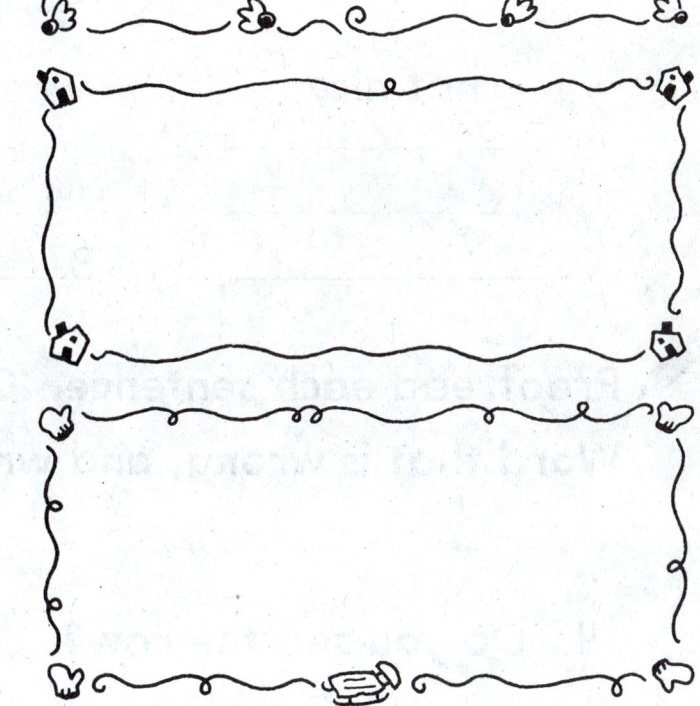

Use one of the circled words in a sentence.

_____
_____
_____
_____

Theme 6: **Animal Adventures** 83

Name _____

Spelling Spree

Week 2
Spelling The Long *e* Sound

Write the Spelling Word for each clue.

Spelling Words

me
see
mean
feet
eat
he

same as I

1. _____

not nice

2. _____

him

3. _____

Proofread each sentence. Circle each Spelling Word that is wrong, and write it correctly.

4. Do you sea the cow? _____

5. It has big fete. _____

6. It likes to eet grass. _____

84   Theme 6: **Animal Adventures**

Name _____

Week 2
Writing Answering a Question

What Happened?

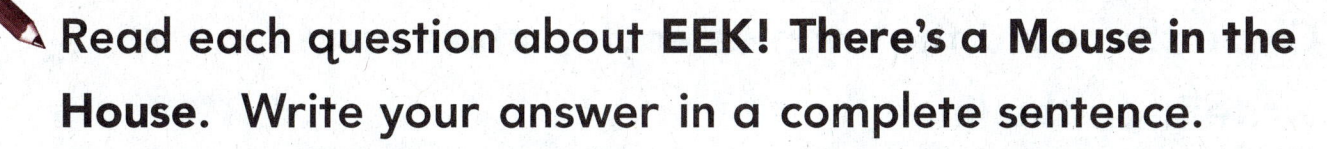

Read each question about **EEK! There's a Mouse in the House.** Write your answer in a complete sentence.

1. What was the first animal that came in the house?

2. How do you think it got in the house?

3. Why did the girl think the elephant could get rid of all the other animals?

Theme 6: **Animal Adventures** 85

Name _____

Week 3

Phonics Vowel Pairs *ai*, *ay*

Words with *ai* or *ay*

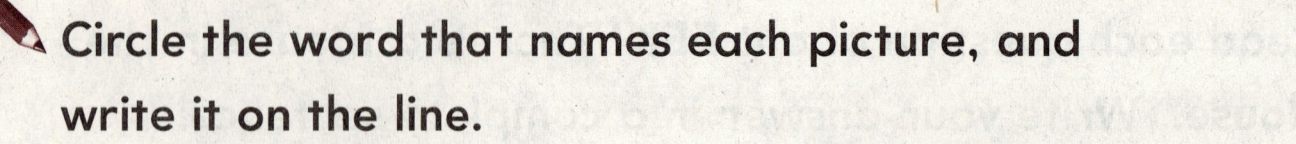

Circle the word that names each picture, and write it on the line.

1.

paint   rain   day

bay   tail   tray

1. _____

2. _____

stain   hay   ray

sail   pail   day

3. _____

4. _____

clay   stay   wait

spray   train   braid

5. _____

6. _____

86   Theme 6: **Animal Adventures**

Week 3

Phonics Vowel Pairs *ai, ay*

Name _____

Words with *ai* or *ay*

Read the words in the box. Then write each word under the word with the same spelling for the long a sound.

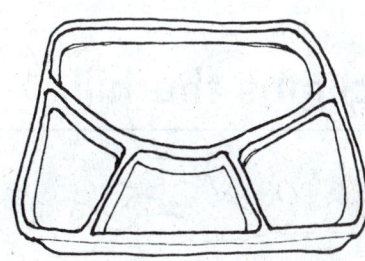

Word Bank

chain
stay
sail
bay
way
rain
day
braid

train

1. _____

3. _____

5. _____

7. _____

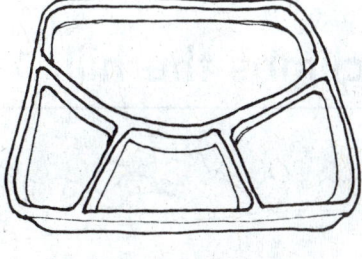

tray

2. _____

4. _____

6. _____

8. _____

Theme 6: **Animal Adventures** 87

Name _____

Week 3

High-Frequency Words

Words to Know

Read each pair of sentences. Circle the sentence that tells about the picture.

1. Evening is here when the sun goes down.

   The horse climbs the hill.

2. The bird goes in its nest.

   The forest has been a home to many animals.

3. It is not far to the lake.

   The animal is hungry.

4. The house is near the forest.

   Soon a horse will come by.

88   Theme 6: **Animal Adventures**

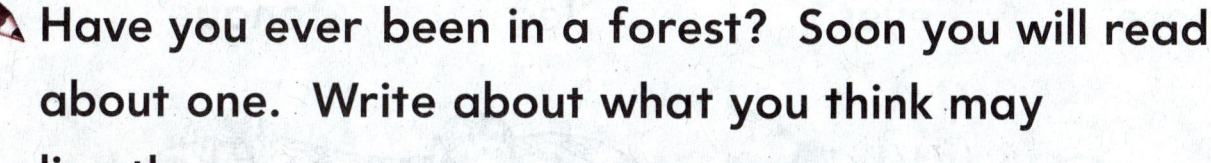

Name _____

Week 3
High-Frequency Words

Words to Know

Read each word in the first list. Draw a line to its opposite.

1. evening   full

2. near   morning

3. hungry   far

4. goes   comes

Have you ever been in a forest? Soon you will read about one. Write about what you think may live there.

_____
_____
_____
_____
_____
_____
_____

Theme 6: **Animal Adventures** 89

Name _____

Week 3

Story Vocabulary *Red-Eyed Tree Frog*

Rain Forest Adventure

Circle the word that names each picture.

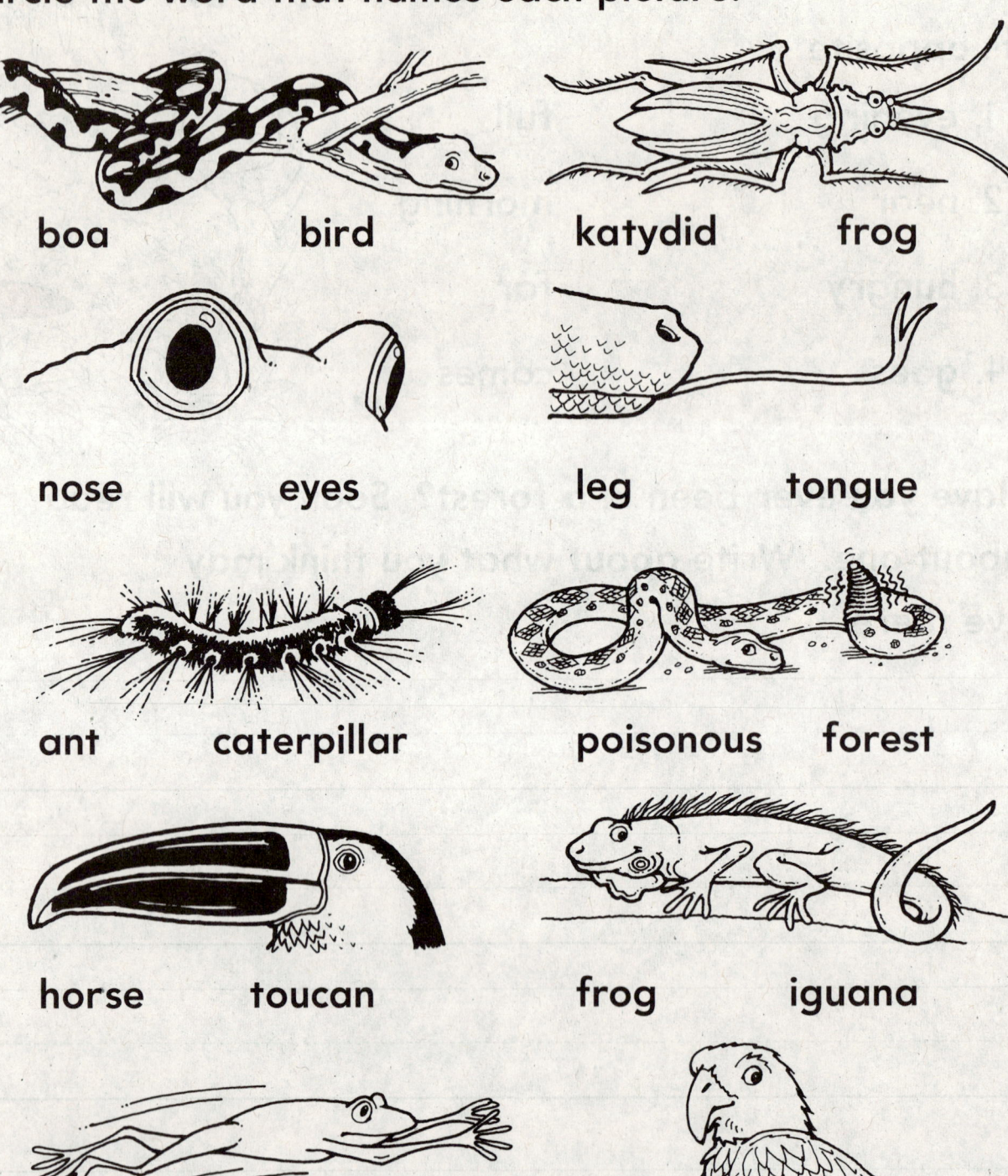

boa   bird   katydid   frog

nose   eyes   leg   tongue

ant   caterpillar   poisonous   forest

horse   toucan   frog   iguana

moves   sleeps   macaw   seal

Theme 6: **Animal Adventures**

Name _____

Week 3

Comprehension Check Red-Eyed Tree Frog

Who's on the Menu?

Color the picture that answers each question.

What does the red-eyed tree frog eat?

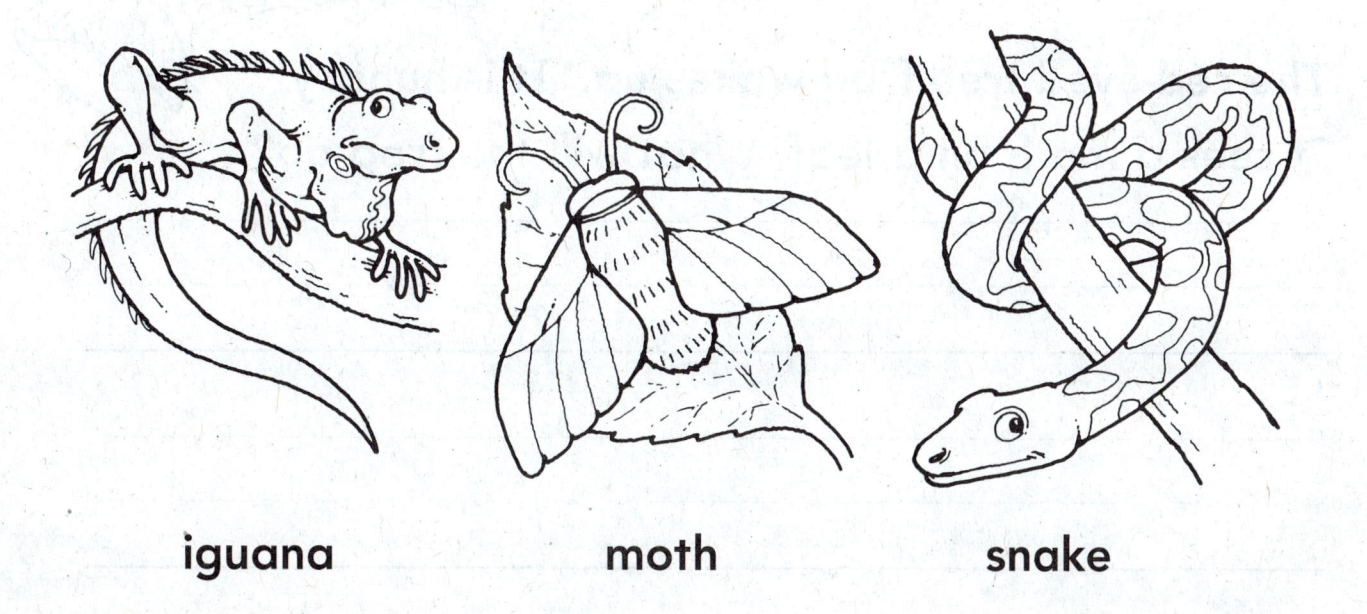

iguana　　　　　moth　　　　　snake

Who would eat the red-eyed tree frog?

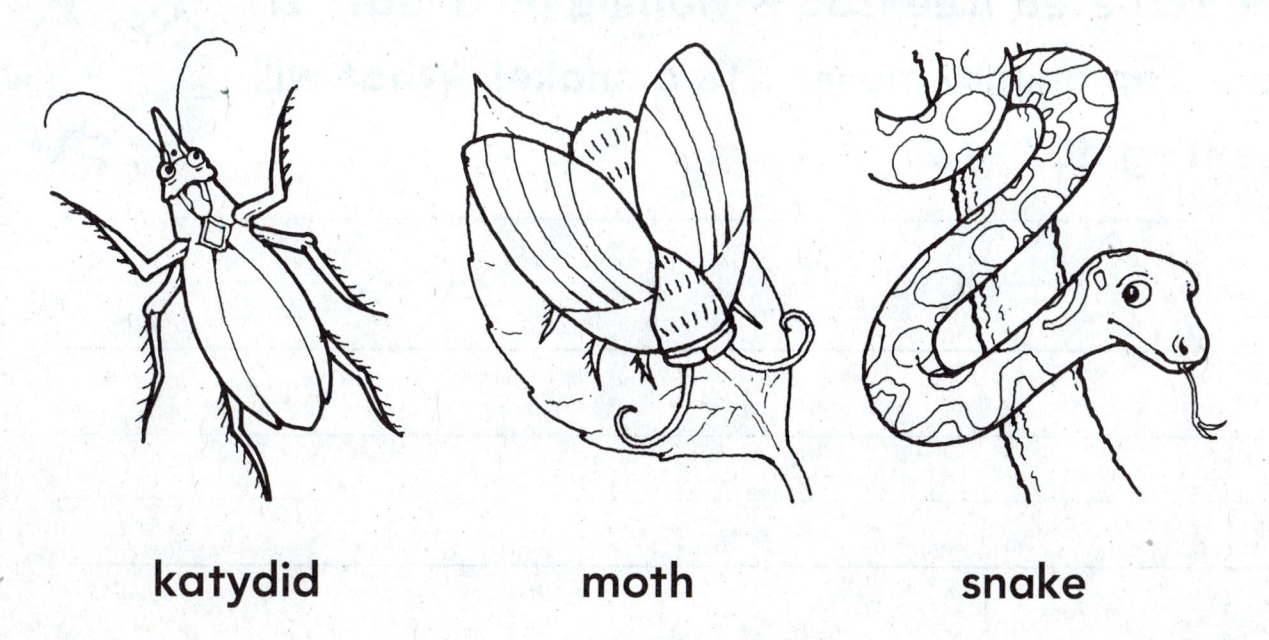

katydid　　　　　moth　　　　　snake

Theme 6: **Animal Adventures**　　91

Name _____

Week 3

Comprehension Making Predictions

What Happens Next?

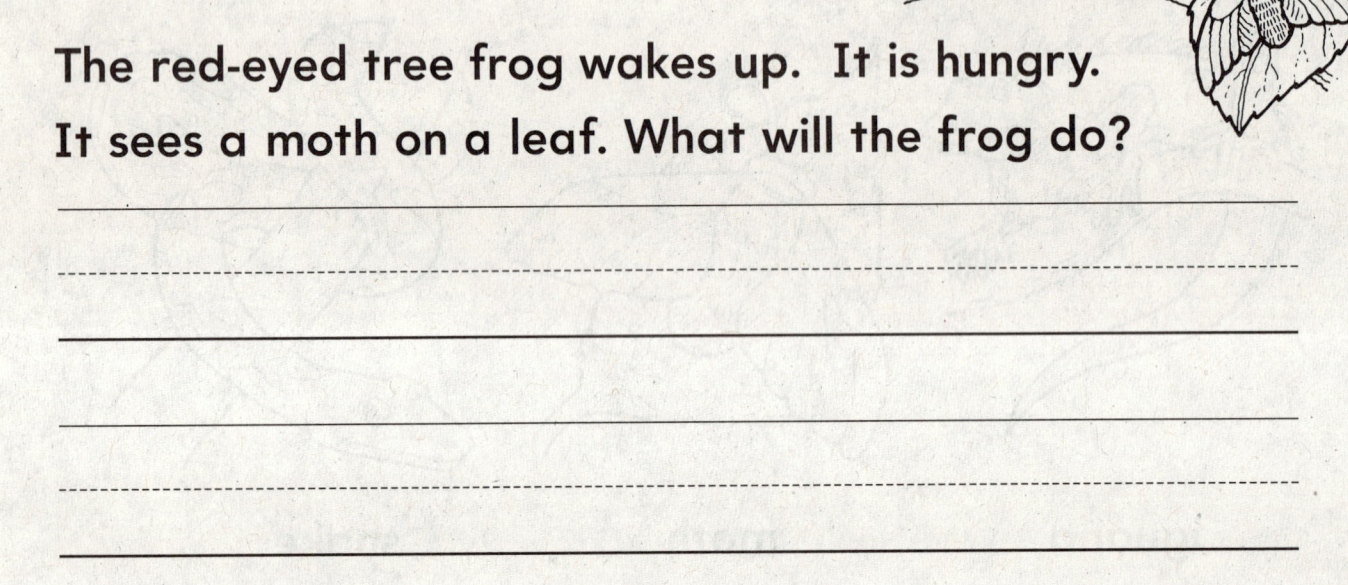

Read each story. Write what you think will happen next.

The red-eyed tree frog wakes up. It is hungry. It sees a moth on a leaf. What will the frog do?

_____
_____
_____
_____

The red-eyed tree frog is waiting on a leaf. It hears an animal move. It's a snake! What will the frog do?

_____
_____
_____
_____

92   Theme 6: **Animal Adventures**

Name _____

Week 3

Spelling The Long *a* Sound Spelled *ay*

The Long *a* Sound Spelled *ay*

Spelling Words

- day
- say
- play
- May
- way
- stay

Read the story. Use the box to help you find and circle words with long *a*.

What a nice day to go out and play. May we go out? We can stay here or go way over there by the trees. What do you say?

Theme 6: **Animal Adventures** 93

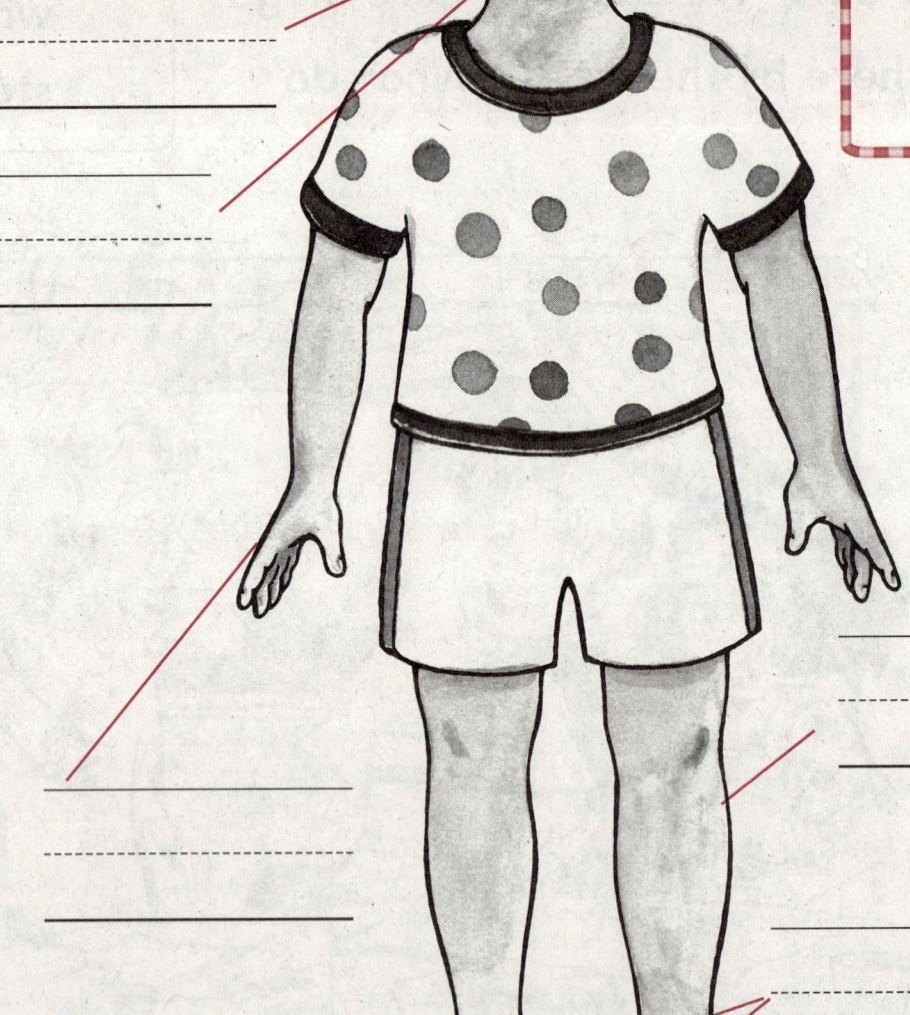

Name _____

Week 3

Vocabulary Parts of the Body

Parts of the Body

Read each word. Label the girl with the words.

Word Bank

nose
neck
leg
feet
hand
teeth

94 Theme 6: **Animal Adventures**

Name _____

Week 3
Grammar Naming Words for One or More

Naming Words

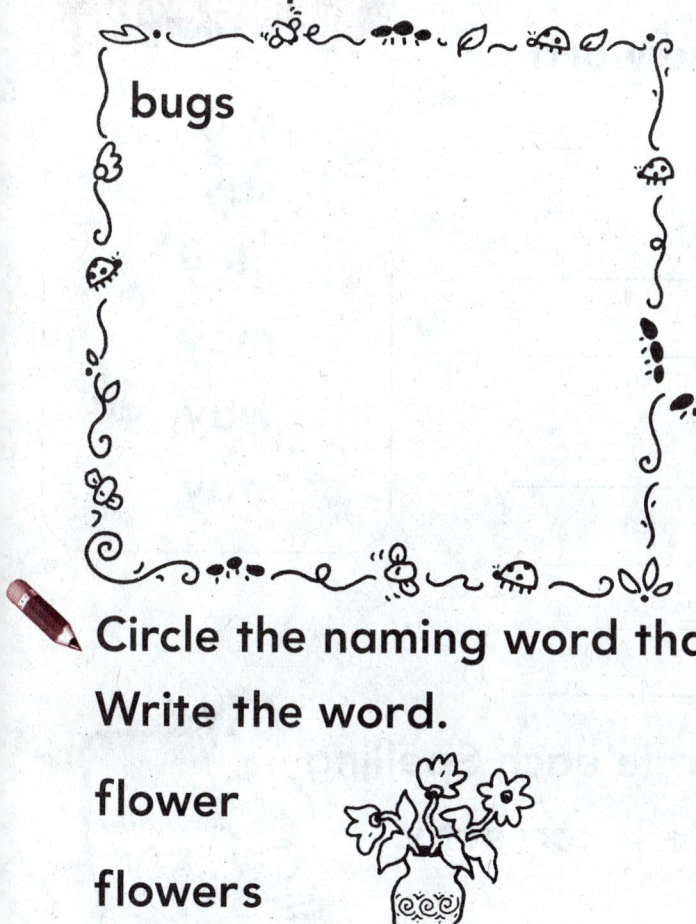

Draw a picture for each word.

bugs

frog

Circle the naming word that matches each picture. Write the word.

flower
flowers

_____

door
doors

_____

girl
girls

_____

sock
socks

_____

Theme 6: **Animal Adventures** 95

Name _____

Week 3

Spelling The Long *a* Sound Spelled *ay*

Spelling Spree

✏️ Write the missing letters to complete each Spelling Word. Write the word.

Spelling Words

day
say
play
may
way
stay

1. st __ __   1. _____

2. w __ __   2. _____

3. d __ __   3. _____

✏️ Proofread each sentence. Circle each Spelling Word that is wrong, and write it correctly.

1. What did you saye?   _____

2. Mae I go out to play? _____

3. Let's palay a game.   _____

96   Theme 6: **Animal Adventures**

Name _____

Week 3

Writing Writing a Summary

Sum It Up!

Think about the story **The Sleeping Pig**.
Write a summary of it.

This story is about _____

_____
_____
_____
_____
_____
_____
_____
_____

Read what you wrote to a friend.

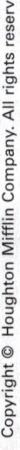

Theme 6: **Animal Adventures** 97

Name _____

Animal Adventures

Taking Tests

Filling in the Blank

Now use what you have learned about taking tests. Answer these fill-in-the-blank questions about **Eek! There's a Mouse in the House**. Look back at the story if you need to. This practice will help you when you take this kind of test.

Read each sentence. Fill in the circle next to the best answer.

1. The girl would like the _____ to chase the rat.

   ○ dog
   ○ cat
   ○ cow

2. The hog _____ but does not chase the dog.

   ○ hops with a mop
   ○ cracks a dish
   ○ eats the cake

Theme 6: **Animal Adventures**   99

Name _____

Filling in the Blank continued

Animal Adventures

Taking Tests

3   When the hen comes in, it _____.

  ○ lays eggs on the table
  ○ gets tangled up
  ○ mops up a mess

4   The _____ comes in from the stable.

  ○ elephant
  ○ sheep
  ○ horse

5   At the end of the story, the _____ is in the house with the mouse.

  ○ cat
  ○ elephant
  ○ cow

100   Theme 6: **Animal Adventures**

Animal Adventures:
Theme 6 Wrap-Up

Spelling Review

Name _____

Spelling Review

Write a Spelling Word next to each number.

Spelling Words

| go | home | me | mean | feet | stay |

1. _____

2. _____

3. _____

4. _____

5. _____

6. _____

Color the mice green next to the long e words.

Color the mice brown next to the long a words.

Color the mice red next to the long o words.

Theme 6: **Animal Adventures** 101

Name _____

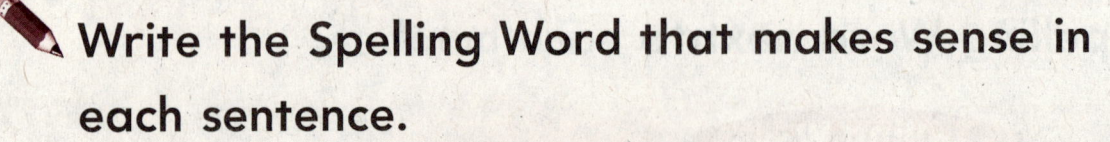

**Animal Adventures:
Theme 6 Wrap-Up**

Spelling Review

Spelling Spree

✏️ Write the Spelling Word that makes sense in each sentence.

Spelling Words

| day | nose | home | eat | feet | play |

1. My friend and I take a walk every _____ .

2. We jump and _____ in the mud.

3. We splash mud with our _____ .

✏️ Proofread each sentence. Circle each Spelling Word that is wrong, and write it correctly.

4. A mole digs a hole for a hom. _____

5. A mole can ete a lot of bugs. _____

6. It has to find bugs with its nos. _____

102 Theme 6: **Animal Adventures**

Name _____

Week 1

Phonics Vowel Pairs *oa, ow*

Words with *oa* and *ow*

Write two words from the box to complete each sentence.

Word Bank

snow
road
goat
toad
crow
boat

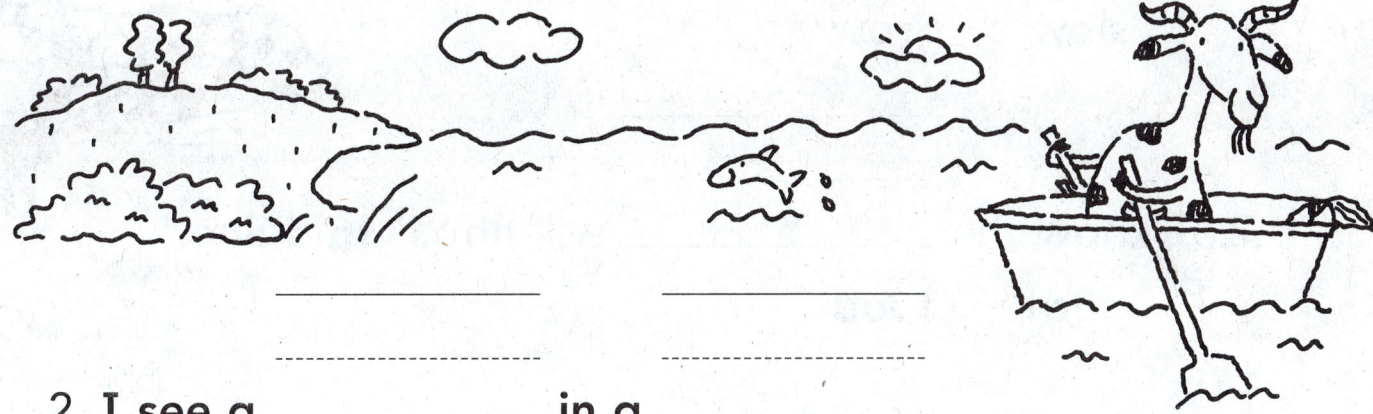

1. I see a _____ in the _____.

2. I see a _____ in a _____.

3. I see a _____ in the _____.

Theme 7: **We Can Work It Out** 103

Name _____

Words with oa and ow

Week 1

Phonics Vowel Pairs *oa, ow*

✏️ **Circle the word that makes sense in each sentence. Write the word.**

1. "Sh! Go _____ ," said Fred.

    slow   grow

2. "I know the _____ will hop," said Sue.

    goat   toad

3. "Now, _____ me where it will go, Sue."

    show   glow

4. "Look! See the toad hop up the _____ ."

    road   boat

104   Theme 7: **We Can Work It Out**

Name _____

Week 1

High-Frequency Words

Words to Know

Fold a piece of paper in half to make a book.
Cut and paste the story parts on the pages in order.
Write your own ending on the last page.

"Do I go this way or that way?" asked Toad.

"I can look at the map again," said Al.
"Look for Big Lake Road."

"We must both look for the road," said Toad.

"Pull the wheel hard so you don't hit that hole!" said Al. "The map is gone, but there is the lake!"

This Way or That Way?

"I want to go to the lake," said Al.

"Let's go, but it's my turn to drive," said Toad.

Theme 7: **We Can Work It Out**

106

Name _____

Week 1

High-Frequency Words

Words to Know

Read the story. Find and circle the words from the box in the story.

Word Bank

| again | both | gone | or |
| want | turn | hard | |

    The cat, the dog, and the bee want to play tag. The cat tags the bee. Now it's the bee's turn, but where has the bee gone? Will the bee tag the cat or the dog? It's hard to do, but the bee tags both the cat and the dog. Then the bee is gone again.

Draw a picture to show what happened.

Theme 7: **We Can Work It Out**   107

Name _____

Week 1

Story Vocabulary *That Toad Is Mine!*

Sort It Out!

Read the words in the box. Write snack words in the lunch box. Write school and home words in the bookcase.

Word Bank

| agree | books | candy bars | crayons | fault |
| food | hoptoad | lemonade | share | toys |

Write the rest of the words.

108 Theme 7: **We Can Work It Out**

Week 1

Comprehension Check *That Toad Is Mine!*

Name _____

And Then What?

✂ Cut out and paste the sentences in order.

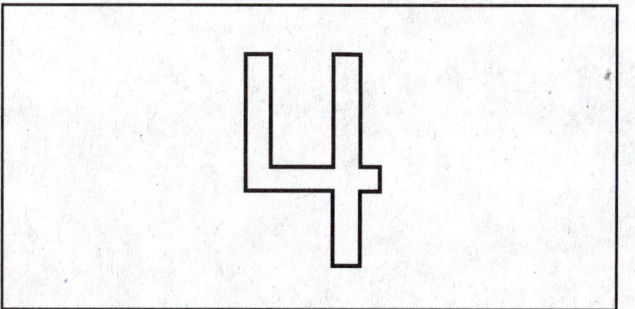

1

2

3

4

The boys get mad.

They see a toad, but they can't agree on how to share it.

They kick a stone until their "mad" is gone.

John and his friend like to share things.

Theme 7: **We Can Work It Out** 109

Name _____

Week 1

Comprehension Problem Solving

What Will They Do?

Read each problem. Write a sentence to tell how you would solve it.

1. Three children want to color their pictures. One of the children doesn't have crayons. What can they do?

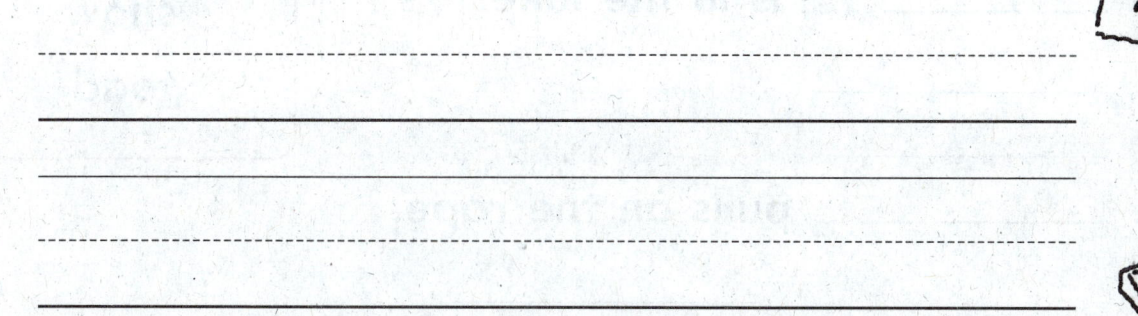

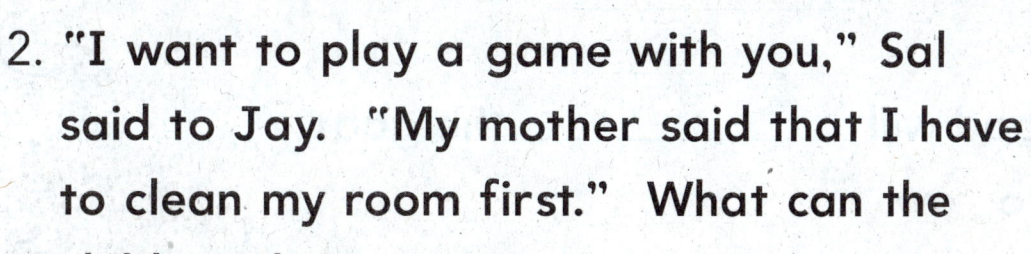

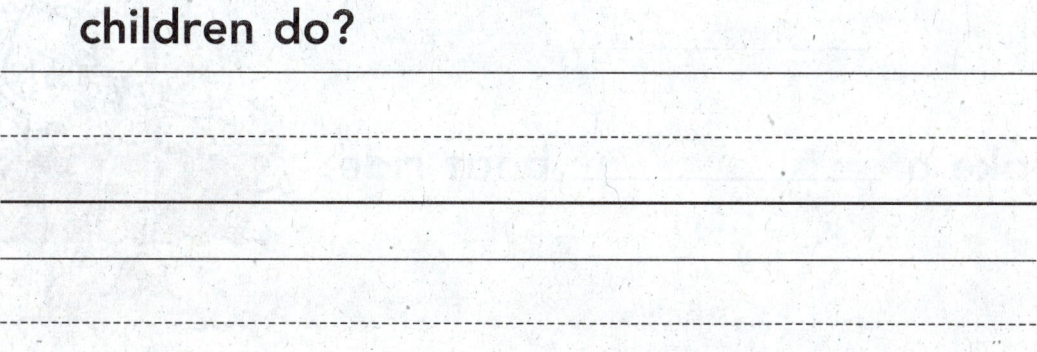

   _____
   _____
   _____
   _____
   _____

2. "I want to play a game with you," Sal said to Jay. "My mother said that I have to clean my room first." What can the children do?

   _____
   _____
   _____
   _____
   _____

Theme 7: **We Can Work It Out** 111

Name _____

More Long o Spellings

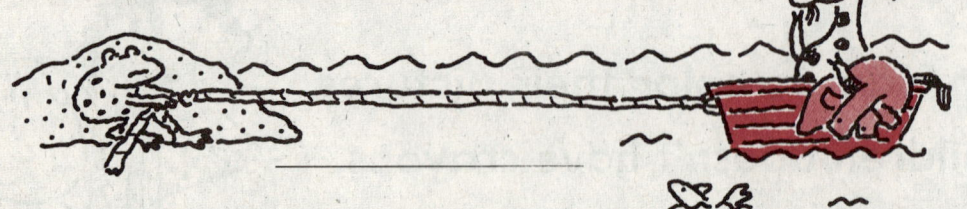

Write a word from the box to complete each sentence.

Spelling Words

boat
slow
coat
grow
show
toad

1. The _____ is in the lake.

2. The _____ pulls on the rope.

3. The goat holds the _____ in the boat.

4. The toad will _____ the goat how to row.

5. They take a _____ boat ride.

6. Soon it will _____ dark.

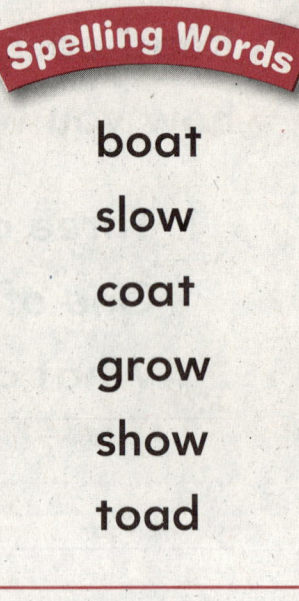

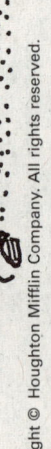

Name _____

Week 1

Vocabulary Categorizing

Sort It Out!

Write color words in the crayon box.
Write animal words in the barn.

Word Bank

| red | pig | dog | pink | green |
| brown | goat | cow | blue | toad |

Theme 7: **We Can Work It Out**   113

Name _____

Week 1

Grammar Special Naming Words

Puzzle Fun

Find each shape that has a special naming word, and color it green.

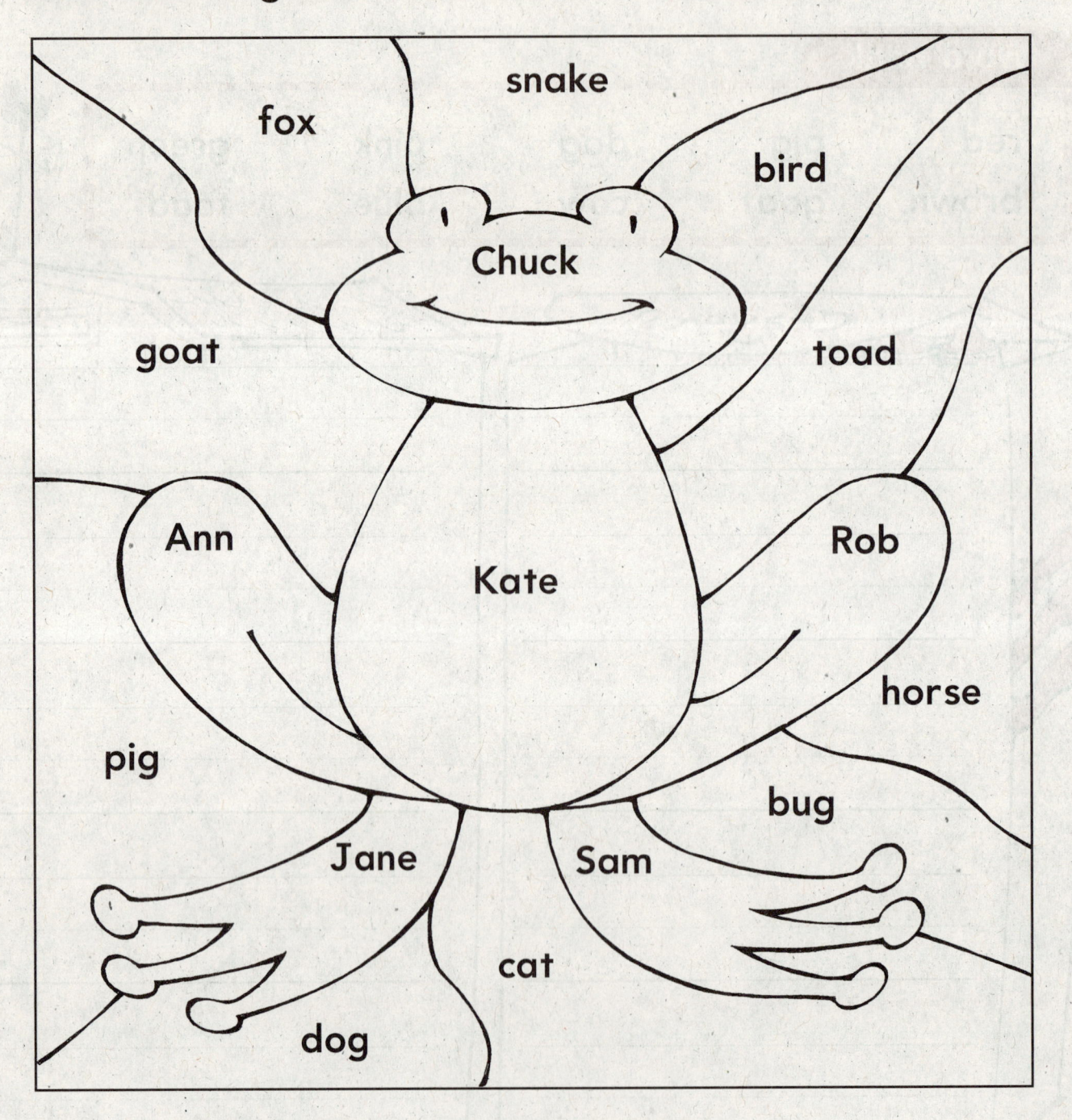

- snake
- fox
- bird
- Chuck
- goat
- toad
- Ann
- Kate
- Rob
- pig
- horse
- Jane
- Sam
- bug
- cat
- dog

114 Theme 7: **We Can Work It Out**

Name _____

Week 1

Spelling More Long *o* Spellings *(oa, ow)*

Spelling Spree

Circle and write the hidden spelling words.

Spelling Words

| boat | slow | coat | grow | show | toad |

rstoad   bslowm   yboatx

1. _____   2. _____   3. _____

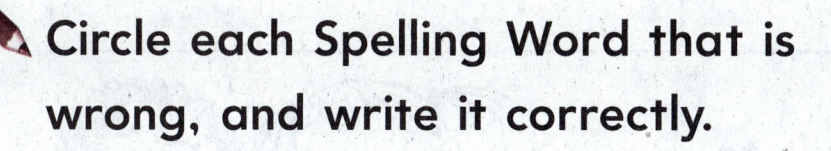

Circle each Spelling Word that is wrong, and write it correctly.

4. Here is a red kote.   _____

5. Cho me that hat.   _____

6. I will gro big.   _____

Theme 7: **We Can Work It Out**   115

Name _____

Week 1

Writing Writing Clearly with Naming Words

We Can Do It!

✏️ Write two naming words in each box.

People	Places
Animals	**Things**

✏️ Use some of the words to write a sentence about how you and a friend share.

_____
_____
_____
_____

116   Theme 7: **We Can Work It Out**

Name _____

Reading-Writing Workshop

Revising Your Story

Revising Your Story

Put a check next to the sentences that tell about your story.

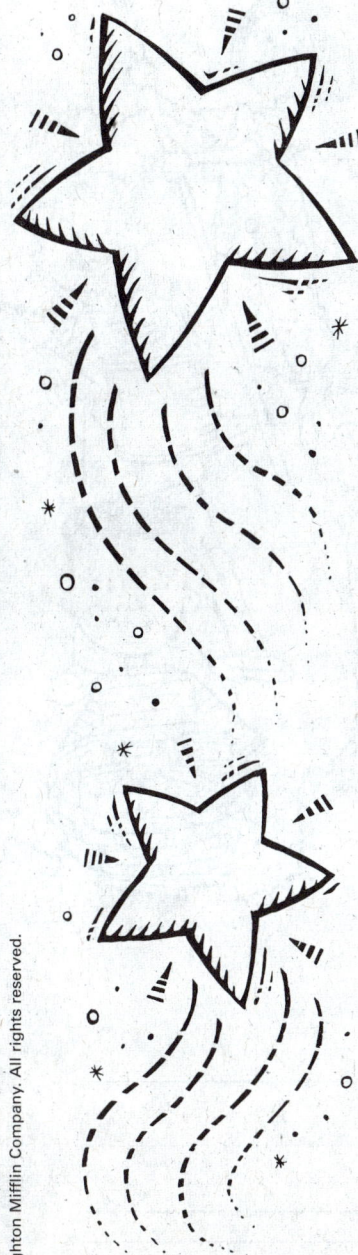

Superstar

☐ My story has a good beginning.
☐ My story has a middle.
☐ My story has a good ending.
☐ My story has a good title.
☐ I used capital letters for people's names.

Rising Star

☐ My story needs a good beginning.
☐ The middle of my story could be better.
☐ My story needs an ending.
☐ I need to add a good title to my story.
☐ I need to fix the way I wrote people's names.

Theme 7: **We Can Work It Out** 117

Name _____

Reading-Writing Workshop

Improving Your Writing

Capitalizing People's Names

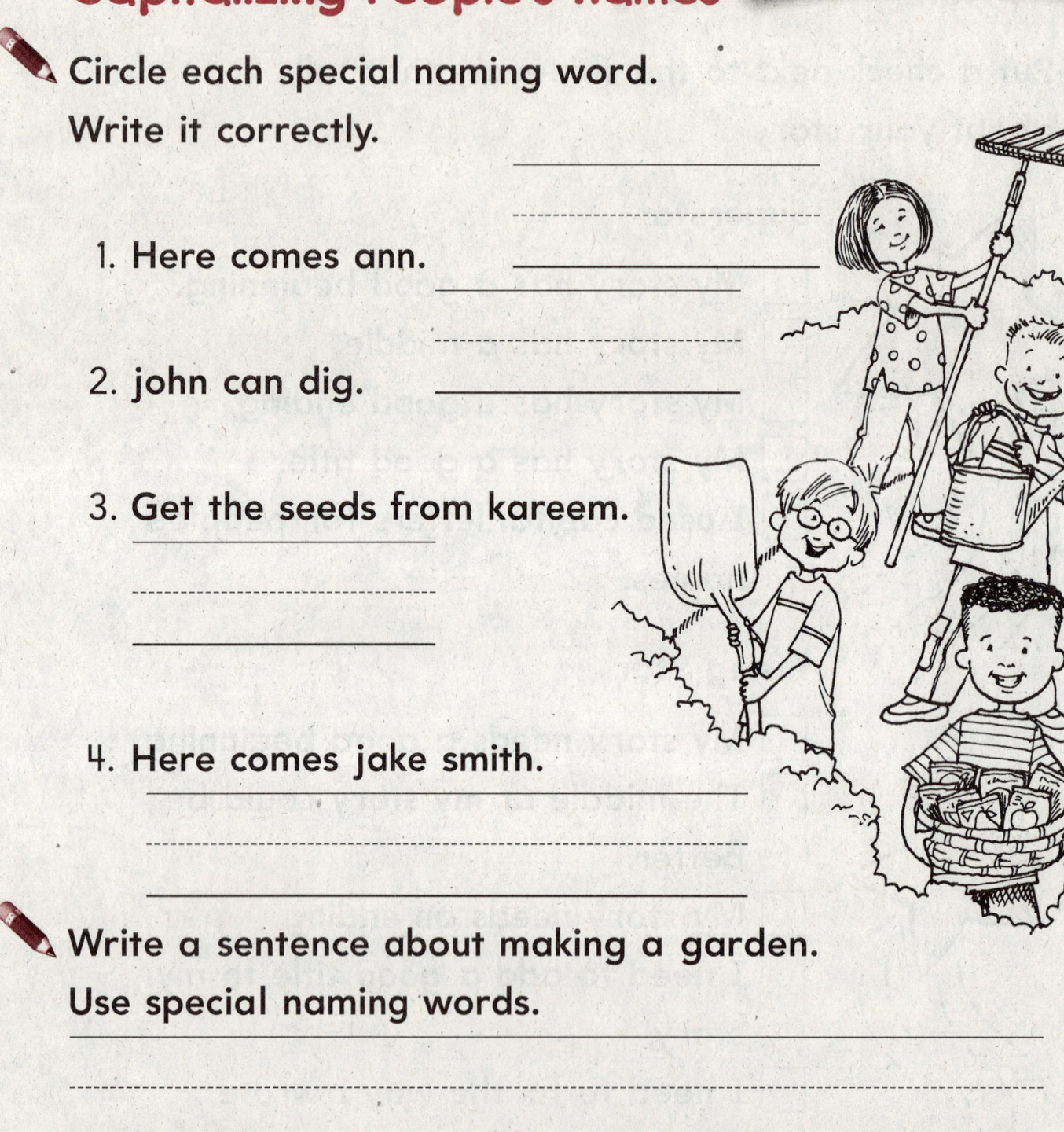

Circle each special naming word. Write it correctly.

1. Here comes ann. _____

2. john can dig. _____

3. Get the seeds from kareem. _____

4. Here comes jake smith. _____

Write a sentence about making a garden. Use special naming words.

_____
_____
_____
_____

118   Theme 7: **We Can Work It Out**

Week 2

Phonics Sound for *oo* as in *book*

Name _____

That Looks Like Fun!

Read the word at the top of the slide.
Write new words as you go down the slide.
The first one is done for you.

Change the **b** in **book** to **t**.

b o o k
t o o k

1. Change the **t** in **took** to **c**.

2. Change the **c** in **cook** to **h**.

3. Change the **h** in **hook** to **l**.

4. Change the **l** in **look** to **br**.

Write a sentence about something good you like to do.

_____

_____

Theme 7: **We Can Work It Out** 119

Name _____

A Good Cook

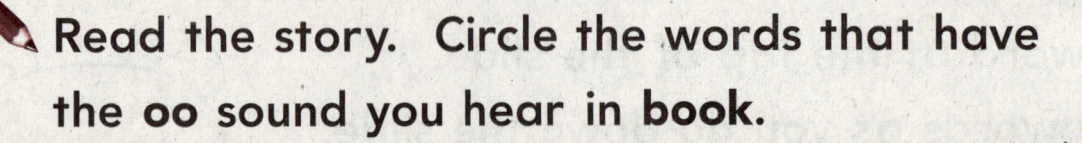

✏️ Read the story. Circle the words that have the **oo** sound you hear in **book**.

Week 2

Phonics Sound for *oo* as in *book*

The cook got a book. She took a look. She stood by the stove. She cooked fast. "Good!" said the cook.

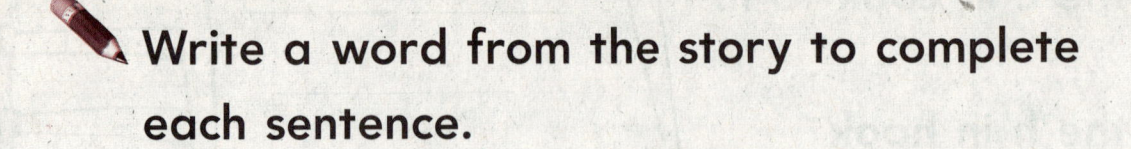

✏️ Write a word from the story to complete each sentence.

The cook took a look at the _____.

"This is a _____ book!" said the cook.

120   Theme 7: **We Can Work It Out**

Week 2

Phonics Compound Words

Name _____

Help Bear Find the Way

Help Bear follow the trail to the forest. Look at each picture. Write a word from the box to complete each compound word.

Word Bank

hop
rain
cake
back
nut

1. pea _____

2. _____ toad

3. _____ bow

4. _____ pack

5. cup _____

Now use one of the compound words in a sentence.
_____
_____

Theme 7: **We Can Work It Out** 121

Week 2

High-Frequency Words

Name _____

Words to Know

Read each pair of sentences. Circle the sentence that goes with the picture.

1. Two little bears have two pails of water.

   Two tall bears come to a path.

2. One tall bear says, "Follow me."

   This pail has the most water.

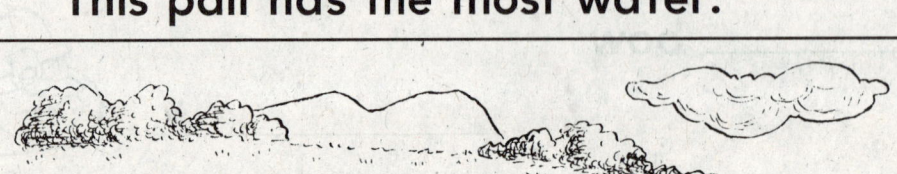

3. Is there any food here?

   Three bears look at the pails.

4. One little bear is afraid of the woods.

   One little bear gets an idea to share.

122   Theme 7: **We Can Work It Out**

Name _____

Words to Know

Write a word from the box to complete each sentence.

Word Bank

afraid
any
follow
most
water
idea

1. I am not _____ of the big, tall dog that looks like a bear.

2. He can _____ me.

3. I don't have _____ food.

4. But I can give him _____.

5. This was a good _____.

6. Now _____ of the water is gone!

Theme 7: **We Can Work It Out** 123

Week 2

Story Vocabulary *Lost!*

Name _____

A Ride to the Top

Read the story. Then answer the question.

This building is in the city. The building is so tall it looks like the top of it disappears! But I don't let it scare me. The friendly man meets us. He tells us not to worry. We take the elevator to the top. We can see the library and the park from up here!

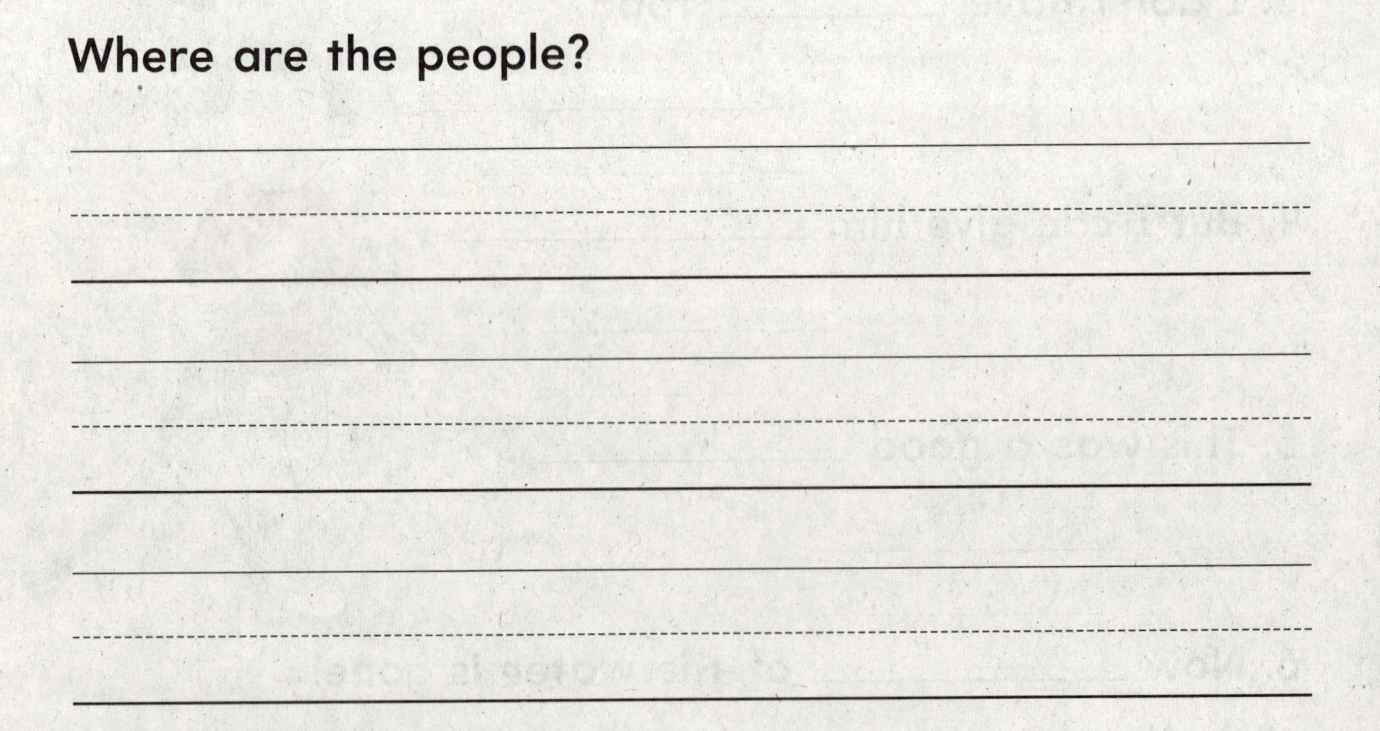

Where are the people?

_____
_____
_____
_____
_____
_____

Theme 7: **We Can Work It Out**

Name _____

Week 2
Comprehension Check *Lost!*

Who Was Lost?

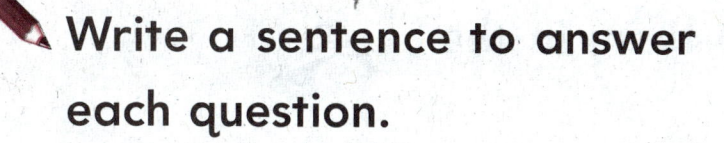

Write a sentence to answer each question.

1. Who was lost in the city?

2. Why did the boy and the bear go to the top of the building?

3. How did the boy get the bear home?

Theme 7: **We Can Work It Out**   125

Name _____

Week 2

Comprehension Sequence of Events

Where Are We?

Read the sentences. Write them in the correct order.

Dad and Dave get home.
Dad and Dave look at the map.
Dad and Dave get lost.

1. First, _____

2. Next, _____

3. Last, _____

126   Theme 7: **We Can Work It Out**

Name _____

The Vowel Sound in *book*

Week 2

Spelling The Vowel Sound in *book*

Write a word from the box to complete each sentence.

Spelling Words

- look
- book
- took
- good
- foot
- cook

1. The cook hurt his _____ .

2. The _____ will rest his foot.

3. The cook will read a _____ .

4. The cook _____ a nap.

5. Now _____ , his foot is fine.

6. It will be a _____ day.

Theme 7: **We Can Work It Out**   127

Name _____

Week 2

Vocabulary Multiple-Meaning Words

Many Meanings

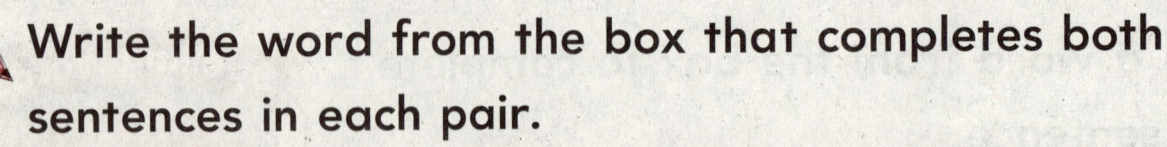

Write the word from the box that completes both sentences in each pair.

Word Bank

| fall | back | left | set |

1. I ____ my book at home. _____

   I write with my ____ hand. _____

2. We rake the leaves in the ____. _____

   I like to ____ into the pile of leaves. _____

3. I have an itch on my ____. _____

   We will send the box ____ to you. _____

4. I have a ____ of books on animals. _____

   Can you ____ that plate down here? _____

Theme 7: **We Can Work It Out**

Name _____

Week 2

Grammar Proper Nouns for Places and Things

Name It!

Read the special naming words. Write a special naming word to go with each picture.

Word Bank

Main Street   Al's Pet Shop
Lost Lake   Redwood City

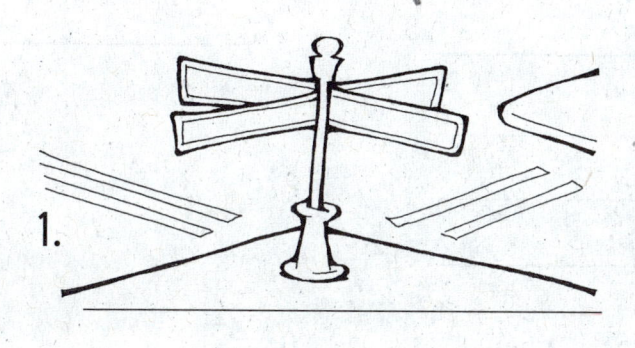

1. _____

2. _____

3. _____

4. _____

Theme 7: **We Can Work It Out**   129

Name _____

Week 2
Spelling The Vowel Sound in *book*

Spelling Spree

✏️ Write the missing letters to complete each Spelling Word. Write the word.

Spelling Words

look
book
took
good
foot
cook

1. f ___ ___ t   _____

2. c ___ ___ k   _____

3. t ___ ___ k   _____

✏️ Proofread each sentence. Circle each spelling word that is wrong, and write it correctly.

4. Luk here.   _____

5. There is the bok.   _____

6. It is a gud book.   _____

130   Theme 7: **We Can Work It Out**

Name _____

Week 2
Writing Writing a Message

Message to a Friend

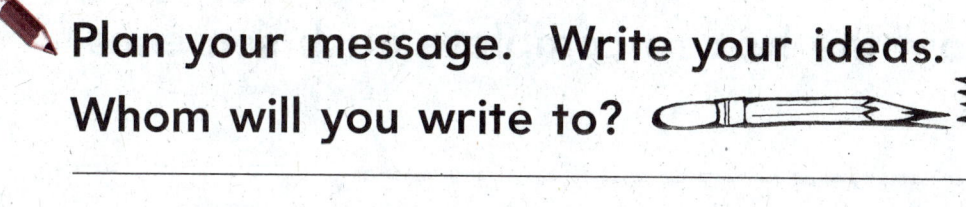

Plan your message. Write your ideas.
Whom will you write to?

_____
_____
_____
_____
_____

What is your message?

_____
_____
_____
_____
_____
_____
_____

Whom is this message from?

_____
_____

Theme 7: **We Can Work It Out** 131

Name _____

Week 3

Phonics Vowel Pairs *oo, ew, ue, ou*

Something New!

Write a word from the box to complete each sentence.

Word Bank

| you | food | new | glue |

1. I drew a picture of _____ .

2. I used paper and some _____ .

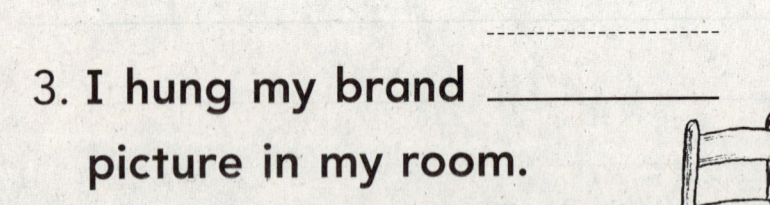

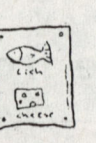

3. I hung my brand _____ picture in my room.

4. Now _____ can make one, too!

132 Theme 7: **We Can Work It Out**

Name _____

Week 3

Phonics Vowel Pairs *oo, ew, ue, ou*

Pig Knew What to Do

Finish each sentence with a word from the Word Bank. Write each word in the correct puzzle boxes.

1. Pig got a ___ pot.
2. He ___ in some glue.
3. He got a few boots, ___.
4. ___ the pot was hot.
5. The ___ was all set.
6. "___ can come eat," said Pig.

Word Bank

threw
You
too
new
Soon
soup

Theme 7: **We Can Work It Out** 133

Name _____

Week 3
Phonics Long *i*: *igh, ie*

A Ride on the Slide

Read the word at the top of the slide. Write new words as you go down the slide. The first one is done for you.

Change the **m** in **might** to **s**.

m i g h t
s i g h t

1. Change the **s** in **sight** to **r**.

2. Change the **r** in **right** to **n**.

3. Change the **n** in **night** to **t**.

4. Change the **t** in **tight** to **l**.

Change the **t** in **tie** to **p** to name something good to eat.

134   Theme 7: **We Can Work It Out**

Name _____

Week 3

High-Frequency Words

Words to Know

Fold a piece of paper in half to make a book. Cut and paste the story parts on the pages in order.
Write your own ending on the last page.

Little Pig did not wear his boots. He left them under his bed. His old shoes get very wet in the rain.

A New House
Miss Pig wants a new house. Little Pig will start to build it.

Wet Little Pig gets a piece of cake from Miss Pig.

Theme 7: **We Can Work It Out** 135

Name _____

Words to Know

Week 3

High-Frequency Words

Read the story. Draw a picture to go with it.

Let's build a snowman! Where shall we start? We can get a very long coat. We'll add a vest under the coat. We can make a top hat from a piece of black paper. The snowman can wear old blue shoes on his feet!

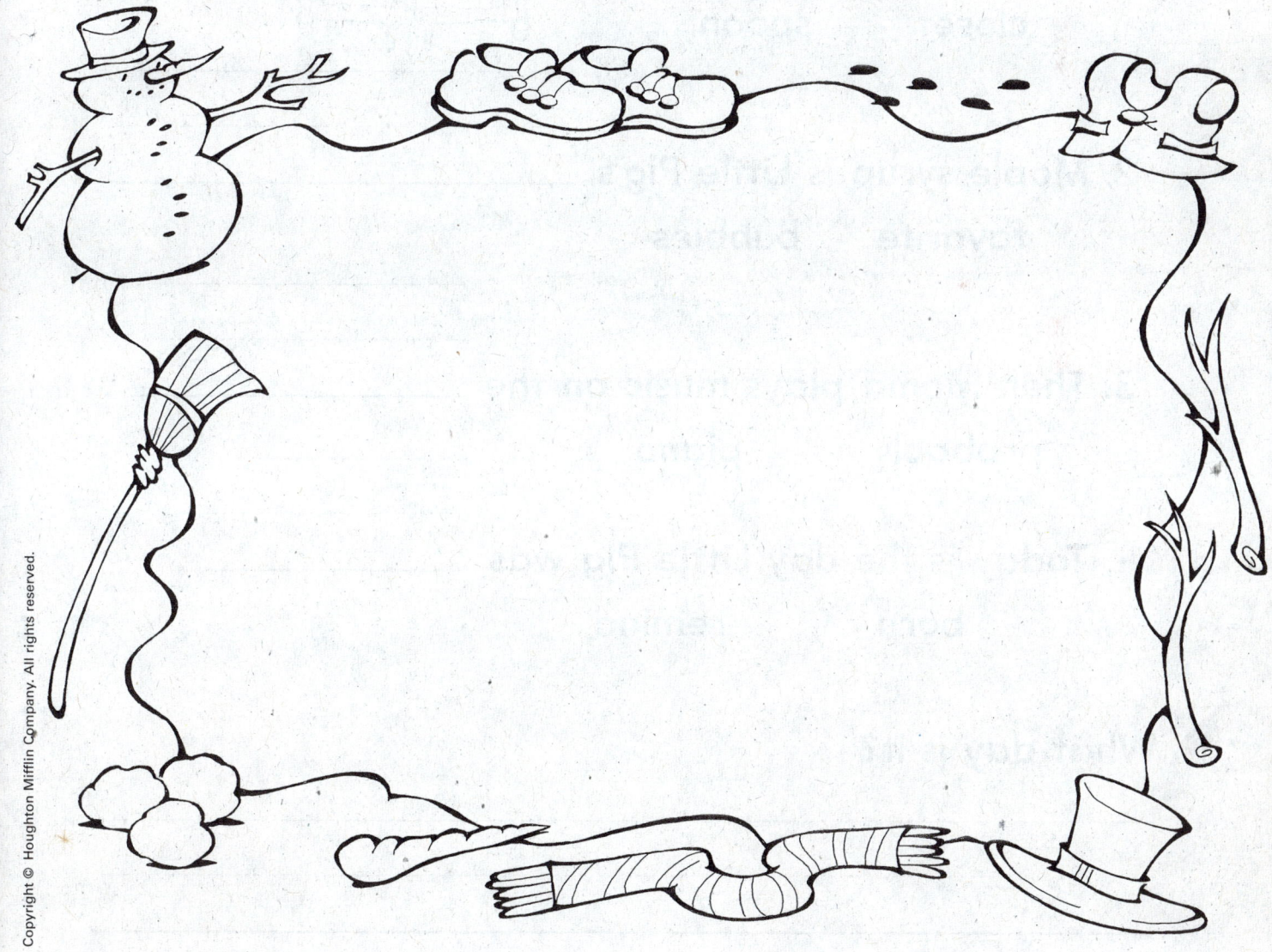

Theme 7: **We Can Work It Out** 137

Name _____

Week 3

Story Vocabulary *If You Give a Pig a Pancake*

A Cake for Little Pig

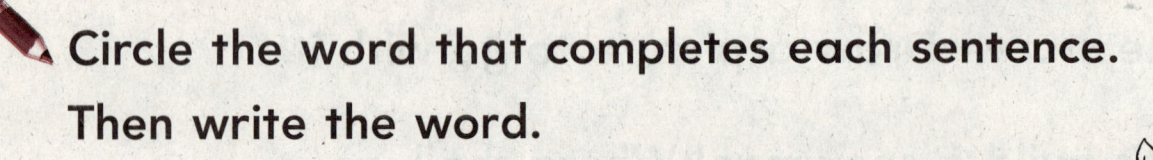

Circle the word that completes each sentence. Then write the word.

1. Mama Pig takes the maple syrup out of the _____.
   closet   spoon

2. Maple syrup is Little Pig's _____.
   favorite   bubbles

3. Then Mama plays music on the _____.
   probably   piano

4. Today is the day Little Pig was _____.
   born   remind

What day is it?

_____

_____

138 Theme 7: **We Can Work It Out**

Name _____

Week 3

Comprehension Check *If You Give a Pig a Pancake*

Why Does the Pig Do Those Things?

Write an answer for each question.

1. Why would the pig want to take a bath?
   _____
   _____
   _____
   _____

2. When would the pig want her picture taken?
   _____
   _____
   _____
   _____

3. If the pig gets glue on her, what would she think of?
   _____
   _____
   _____
   _____

Theme 7: **We Can Work It Out**

Week 3

Comprehension Fantasy and Realism

Name _____

Real or Make-Believe?

Read each sentence.

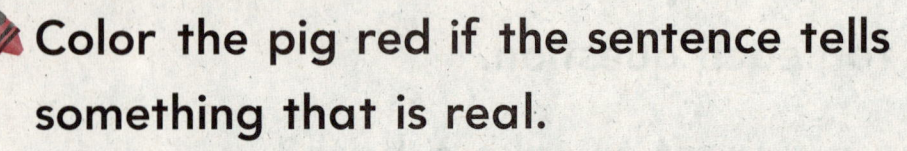

Color the pig red if the sentence tells something that is real.

Color the pig blue if the sentence tells something that is make-believe.

1. Pigs sit in mud.

2. Pigs can sing.

3. Pigs read books.

4. Pigs have four legs.

5. Pigs like to cut out pictures.

6. Pigs fly.

7. Pigs eat a lot.

8. Pigs live in pens.

Name _____

Week 3

Spelling The Vowel Sound in *moon*

Words with *oo* as in *moon*

Spelling Words

too
zoo
moon
food
soon
room

Write the word from the box that completes each sentence.

1. I see the _____ .

2. I see a bird in my _____ .

3. I'll give it some _____ .

4. I'll eat some, _____ .

5. _____ it will be morning.

6. That bird can go back to the _____ .

Theme 7: **We Can Work It Out** 141

Name _____

Week 3

Vocabulary Syllabication

Listen for the Beat

Read each word and clap for each syllable. If the word has one syllable, write it on the barn. If the word has two syllables, write it on the doghouse.

Word Bank

| pig | children | morning | follow |
| bath | you | duck | pancake |

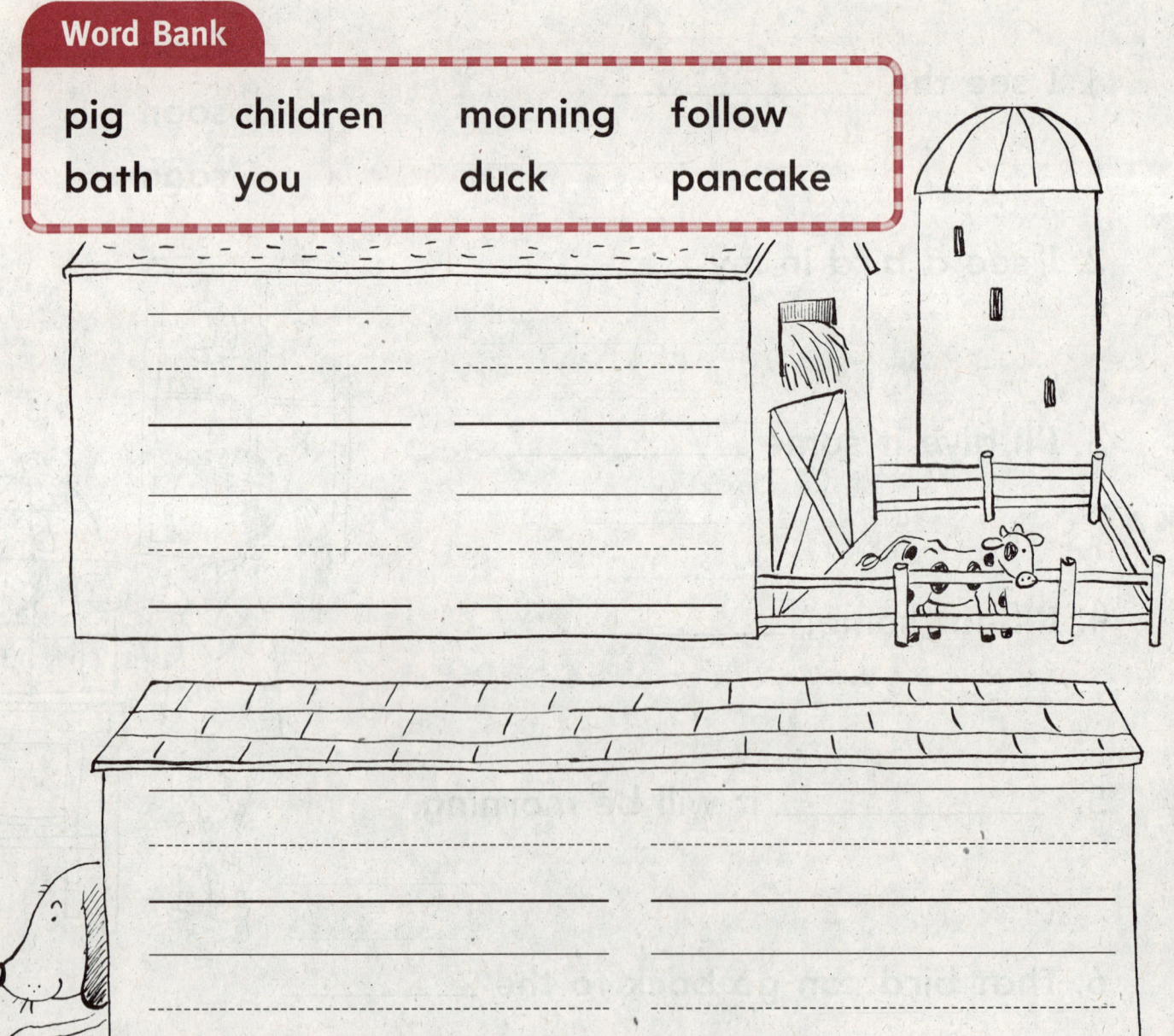

142 Theme 7: **We Can Work It Out**

Name _____

Week 3

Grammar Pronouns

Word Match

Draw a line from each naming word to the word that can take its place. Write each word.

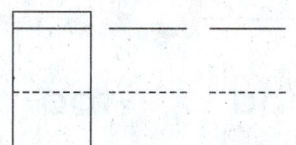

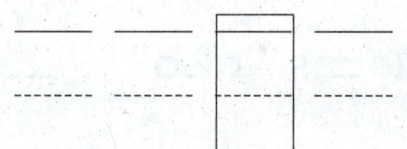

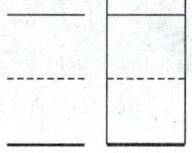

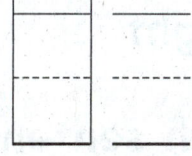

1.  **cats** — She

2.  **Mike** — they

3.  **Ann** — it

4. 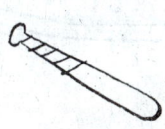 **bat** — he

Write the letter from each box to make a word that answers the question.

Who can play with Ann and Mike? _____

Theme 7: **We Can Work It Out**   143

Name _____

Week 3

Spelling The Vowel Sound in *moon*

Spelling Spree

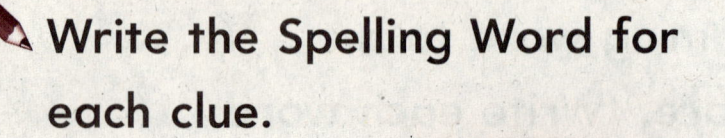

Write the Spelling Word for each clue.

Spelling Words

| zoo | food | too | moon | room |

1. Means "also" _____

2. Means "a home for animals" _____

3. Means "something shiny at night" _____

Proofread each sentence. Circle each Spelling Word that is wrong, and write it correctly.

4. Look at that fod. _____

5. It is all over this rom. _____

144 Theme 7: **We Can Work It Out**

Name _____

Week 3

Writing Writing an Invitation

Please Come!

Write words to finish the invitation.

Come to a Birthday Party!

Dear _____,

Day: _____

Time: _____

Where: _____

_____ is giving the party.

Theme 7: **We Can Work It Out** 145

We Can Work It Out
Taking Tests

Name _____

Writing a Personal Response

Now use what you have learned about taking tests. Write your answer to the question. Then see how you might make your answer better. This practice will help you when you take this kind of test.

In the story **If You Give a Pig a Pancake**, the girl gives the pig a pancake. The pig wants more. Have you given something to someone who said they wanted more? Write about what you would say to that person.

Name _____

Writing a Personal Response

continued

✏️ Read the answer that you wrote on page 147. Check each box that tells about your answer.

- ☐ My sentences answer the question.
- ☐ My sentences tell what I think.
- ☐ My sentences have interesting details.

✏️ If you did not check a box, you can make your answer better. Make your changes here.

Name _____

**We Can Work It Out:
Theme 7 Wrap-Up**
Spelling Review

Spelling Review

✏️ Write the Spelling Words.

Spelling Words

| toad | show | book | too | foot | moon |

1. _____ 2. _____

3. _____ 4. _____

5. _____ 6. _____

✏️ Circle the words with the long **o** sound. Put a check by the words with the vowel sound in **cool**. Draw a smile by the words with the vowel sound in **hook**.

Theme 7: **We Can Work It Out** 149

Name _____

**We Can Work It Out:
Theme 7 Wrap-Up**
Spelling Review

Spelling Spree

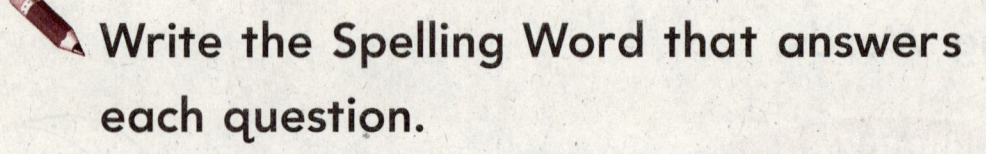

Write the Spelling Word that answers each question.

Spelling Words

toad
look
grow
coat
good
zoo

1. With sun and water, what can a plant do?

   _____

2. Where can you see a lot of animals?

   _____

3. What can jump and eat bugs?

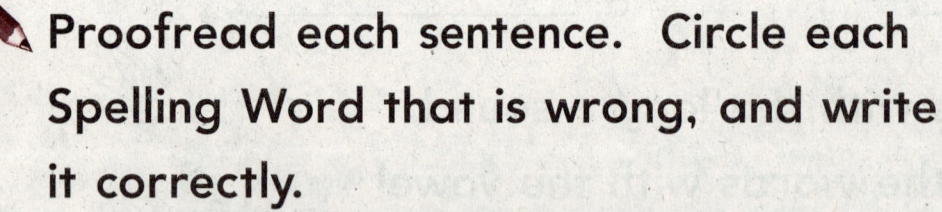

   _____

Proofread each sentence. Circle each Spelling Word that is wrong, and write it correctly.

4. Can you help me luk for my dog?

   _____

5. Boots is a gud dog.

   _____

6. He has spots on his cote.

   _____

150   Theme 7: **We Can Work It Out**

Name _____

A Fine Time!

Week 1

Phonics Base Words with Endings -s, -ed, -ing

Circle and write the correct word to complete each sentence.

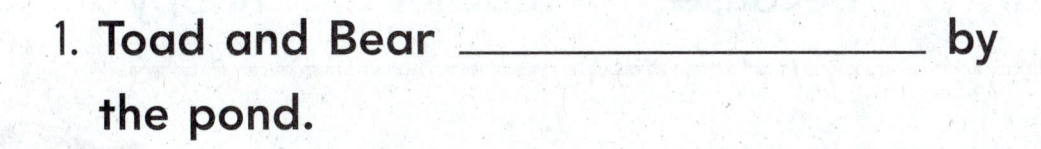

1. Toad and Bear _____ by the pond.

   playing   played

2. Ant _____ at the food.

   looked   looking

3. "Why is Ant _____ at the food?" asked Toad.

   peeking   peeks

4. "Ant _____ to eat!" said Bear.

   wanting   wants

Theme 8: **Our Earth**   151

Name _____

Week 1
High-Frequency Words

Words to Know

Write a word from the box to complete each sentence.

Word Bank

| tiny | part | because | teacher | happy |

1. Our _____ tells us about plants.

2. Plants grow _____ they get sun.

3. We draw each _____ of a plant.

4. It has little, _____ seeds.

5. We feel _____ drawing plants.

152 Theme 8: **Our Earth**

Name _____

Week 1

High-Frequency Words

Words to Know

Read each pair of sentences. Circle the sentence that tells about the picture.

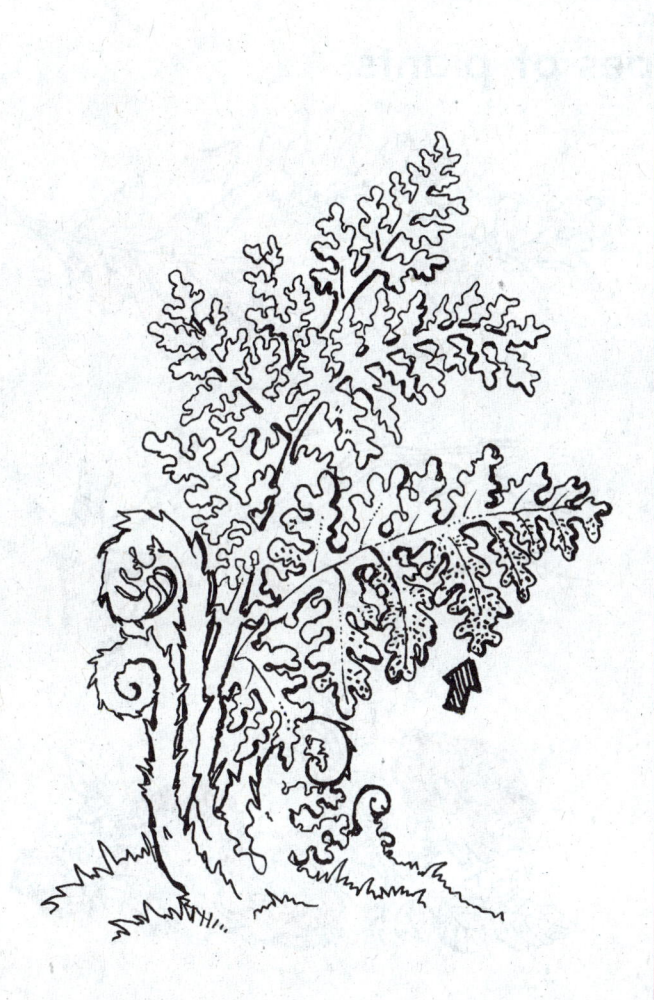

I feel happy when I draw cars.

Tiny seeds are part of this plant.

Plants grow because they get water and sun.

Our teacher tells us about frogs.

Theme 8: **Our Earth**   153

Name _____

Week 1

Story Vocabulary *The Forest*

Interesting Plants

Read each sentence Draw a line from the sentence to the picture it goes with.

There are many different types of plants.

1. Some plants have beautiful flowers.

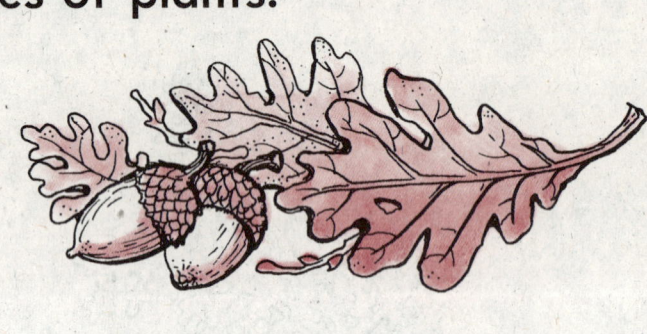

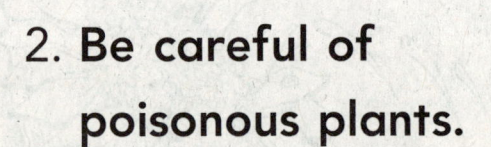

2. Be careful of poisonous plants.

3. Some trees have long branches.

4. Acorns are nuts from the oak tree.

154 Theme 8: **Our Earth**

Name _____

Week 1

Comprehension Check *The Forest*

A Forest Visit

Read the directions and write the answers.

1. Name three things that make their homes in the forest.

   _____
   _____
   _____
   _____
   _____

2. Name one thing to be careful about in the forest.

   _____
   _____
   _____

Theme 8: **Our Earth**   155

Name _____

Week 1

Comprehension Skill
Categorize and Classify

Forest Life

Look at the picture. Write in the correct box the names of the things you see.

Animals

_____
_____
_____
_____
_____

Plants

_____
_____
_____
_____
_____

156 Theme 8: **Our Earth**

Name _____

Adding -s to Naming Words

Week 1

Spelling Adding -s to Naming Words

✏ Write a word from the box to complete each sentence.

Word Bank

| cup | cups | frog | frogs | tree | trees |

1. Two fig _____ grow outside.

2. One oak _____ grows, too.

3. Two blue _____ are there.

4. I see three _____ hop.

5. What is in the blue _____?

6. It is my pet _____!

Theme 8: Our Earth   157

Name _____

Week 1

Vocabulary Compound Words

Match It Up!

Cut out and paste each word card next to a word to make a compound word.

1. **water** [ ]

2. **row** [ ]

3. **bird** [ ]

4. **drum** [ ]

5. **draw** [ ]

stick

bath

string

boat

fall

Theme 8: **Our Earth** 159

Name _____

Week 1

Grammar Action Words

Busy Times

Draw a line from each picture to the action word that goes with it. Write each action word.

1.   eat _____

2.   dig _____

3.   swim _____

4.   sit _____

5.   fly _____

Theme 8: **Our Earth**   161

Name _____

Week 1
Spelling Adding -s to Naming Words

Spelling Spree

Circle and write the hidden Spelling Words.

Spelling Words

| cup | cups | frog | frogs | tree | trees |

1. lcupfa _____

2. gtreec _____

3. rifrog _____

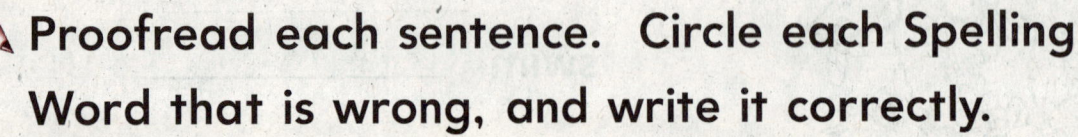

Proofread each sentence. Circle each Spelling Word that is wrong, and write it correctly.

4. Birds live in the treas . _____

5. Frugs live in the pond. _____

6. I have two cps. _____

162 Theme 8: **Our Earth**

Name _____

Week 1

Writing Learning Log

My Learning Log

- Write some facts about **The Forest**.
- Draw pictures to go with the facts.

Animals

Trees

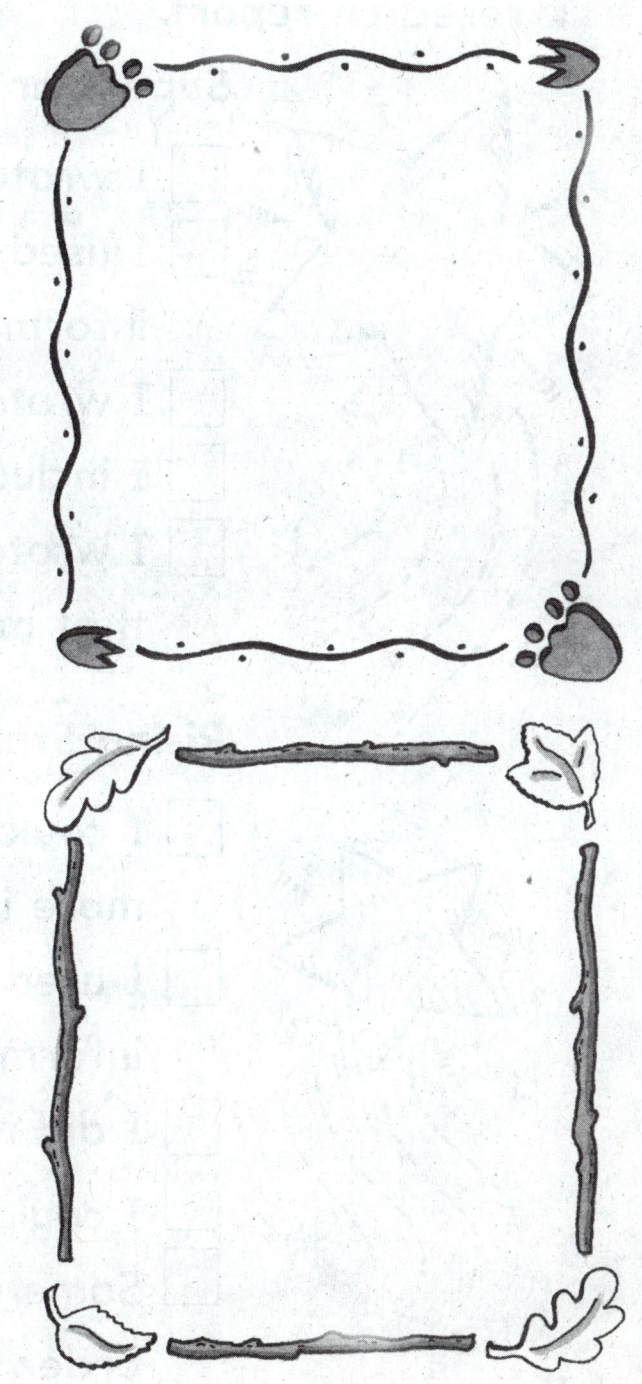

Theme 8: **Our Earth** 163

Name _____

Reading-Writing Workshop

Revising Your Research Report

Revising Your Research Report

✏️ Check the sentences that tell about your research report.

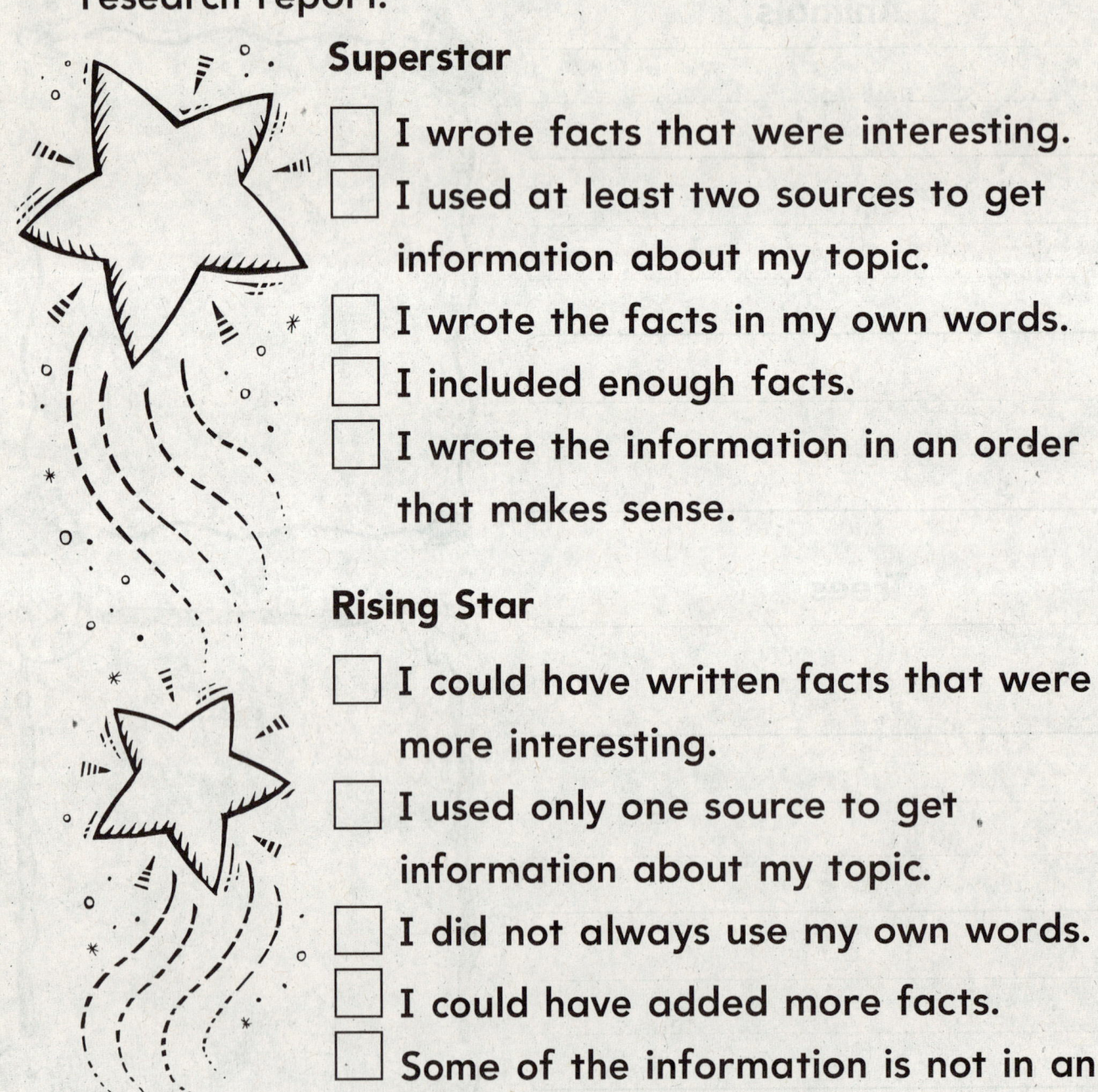

Superstar

- ☐ I wrote facts that were interesting.
- ☐ I used at least two sources to get information about my topic.
- ☐ I wrote the facts in my own words.
- ☐ I included enough facts.
- ☐ I wrote the information in an order that makes sense.

Rising Star

- ☐ I could have written facts that were more interesting.
- ☐ I used only one source to get information about my topic.
- ☐ I did not always use my own words.
- ☐ I could have added more facts.
- ☐ Some of the information is not in an order that makes sense.

Theme 8: **Our Earth**

Name _____

Reading-Writing Workshop

Improving Your Writing

Capitalizing Names

Circle each word that is wrong. Write it correctly.

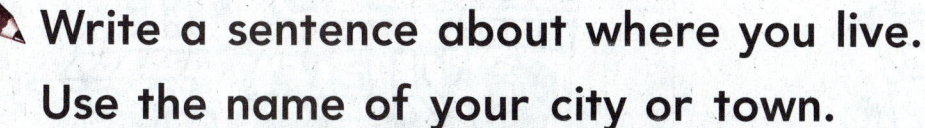

1. We went to a town called davis.

2. Our cat, boots, stayed at home.

3. The bus took us to sea street.

4. I saw a dog called wags.

Write a sentence about where you live. Use the name of your city or town.

Theme 8: **Our Earth**   165

Week 2

Phonics Vowel Pairs *ou, ow*

Name _____

Downtown!

Read the sentences. Write each word in dark print below the picture it names.

There is a funny **clown**.
She runs through the **town**.
There is a little **mouse**.
It runs to its tiny **house**.

1. _____

2. _____

3. _____

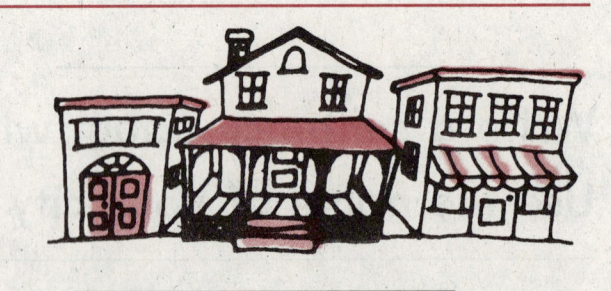

4. _____

166   Theme 8: **Our Earth**

Name _____

Week 2
Phonics Vowel Pairs *ou, ow*

A Hike in the Woods

Circle the word that makes sense in each sentence. Write the word.

_____

1. We hike _____ the trail.

   found   down

_____

2. We do not _____.

   shout   now

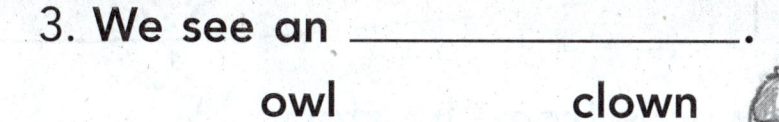

_____

3. We see an _____.

   owl   clown

_____

4. We see a _____ run by.

   flower   mouse

Theme 8: **Our Earth**   167

Week 2

Phonics Syllabication

Name _____

Something Funny!

✏ Read the story. Circle the two-syllable words.

"Follow me," said Big Mouse to Little Mouse.

"Let's eat that oatmeal," said Big Mouse.

The mice ate. What a funny sight!

✏ Write the two-syllable words from the story.

1. _____ 2. _____

3. _____ 4. _____

168 Theme 8: **Our Earth**

Name _____

Week 2

High-Frequency Words

Words to Know

Fold a piece of paper in half to make a book.
Cut and paste the story parts on the pages in order.
Write your own ending on the last page.

1

Always warm up your arms and legs.
One, two, three, four.

2

Stretch your body.
Five, six, seven, eight.

3

Ready! Set! Go!

Theme 8: **Our Earth**   169

Name _____

Week 2

High-Frequency Words

Words to Know

Write a word from the box to complete each sentence.

Word Bank

| eight | warm | ready | body |

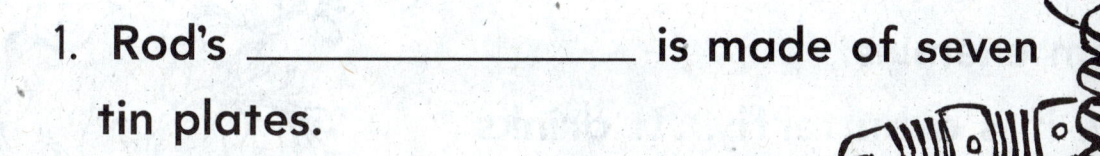

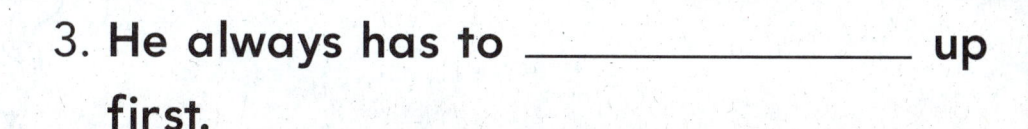

1. Rod's _____ is made of seven tin plates.

2. He has _____ arms.

3. He always has to _____ up first.

4. Then he is _____ to pick up trash!

Theme 8: **Our Earth** 171

Name _____

Week 2

Story Vocabulary Butterfly

Something to See

Read the story.

See the caterpillar in its suit of stripes. Its stripes tell birds, "Danger! I don't taste good!"

It is changing every day. It makes a pouch, or chrysalis. This keeps it safe from enemies.

Now it is a butterfly. It drinks nectar from orange flowers.

Draw a picture to go with the story.

Name _____

Growing and Changing

✏️ Look at the picture. Circle what happened next. Write a sentence to tell about it.

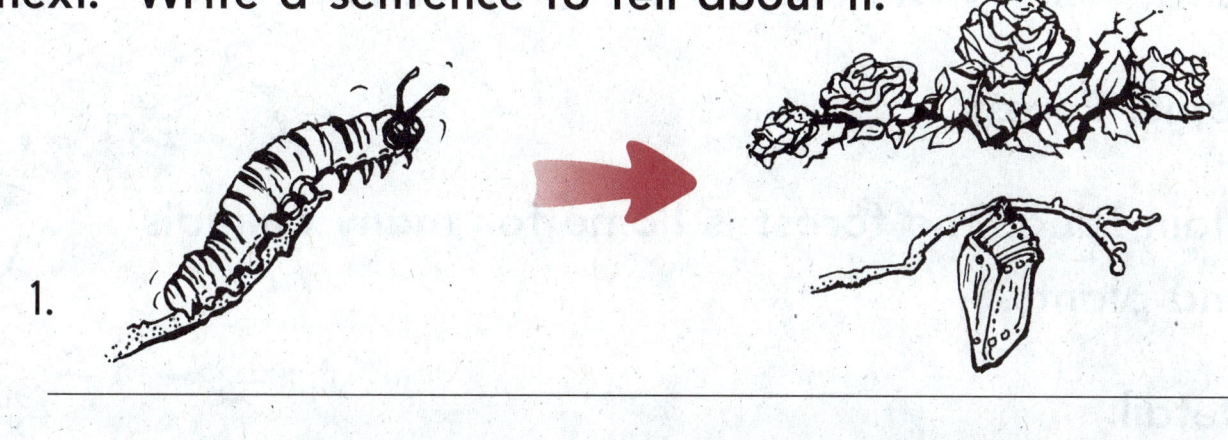

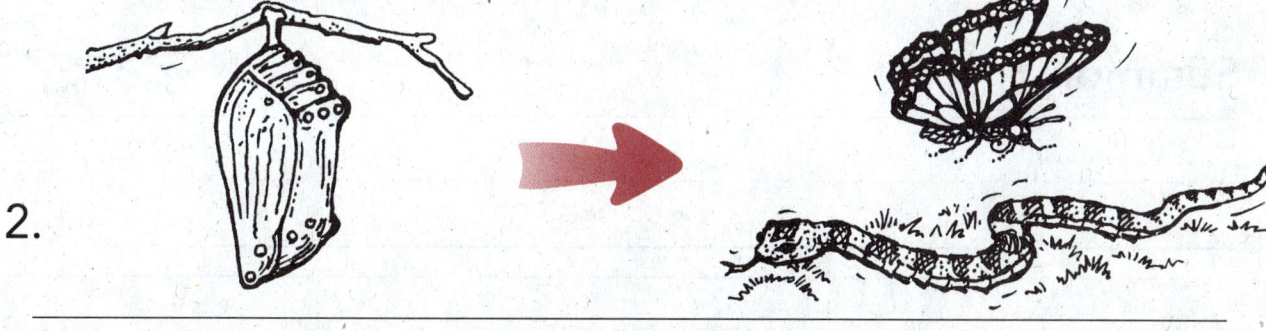

1.

_____
_____
_____

2.

_____
_____
_____

Week 2

Comprehension Check
Butterfly

Theme 8: **Our Earth**   173

Name _____

A Big Change!

Think about **The Forest**. Read the topic and main idea. Then write one detail and a summary.

Topic: Forest

Main Idea: The forest is home for many animals and plants.

Detail:
_____
_____
_____
_____

Summary:
_____
_____
_____
_____

Week 2

Comprehension Topic, Main Idea, and Details/ Summarizing

Name _____

The Vowel Sound in *cow*

Write a Spelling Word to complete each sentence.

Spelling Words

| cow | house | out | down | now | found |

1. This is a crowded _____.

2. A _____ lives here.

3. The cow is packing a bag _____.

4. She goes _____.

5. The cow walks _____ the hill.

6. She has _____ a new home!

Name _____

What Am I?

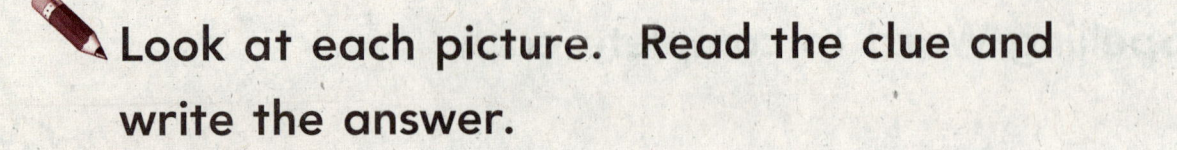

Look at each picture. Read the clue and write the answer.

Word Bank

nectar   chrysalis   butterfly   egg

1. I am a round shell!

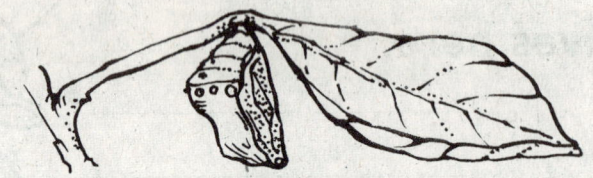

2. I am a pouch for a caterpillar.

3. I have four wings.

4. I am the part of a flower the butterfly sips.

Week 2
Vocabulary Science Words

176 Theme 8: **Our Earth**

Name _____

Week 2

Grammar Present Tense

Right Now!

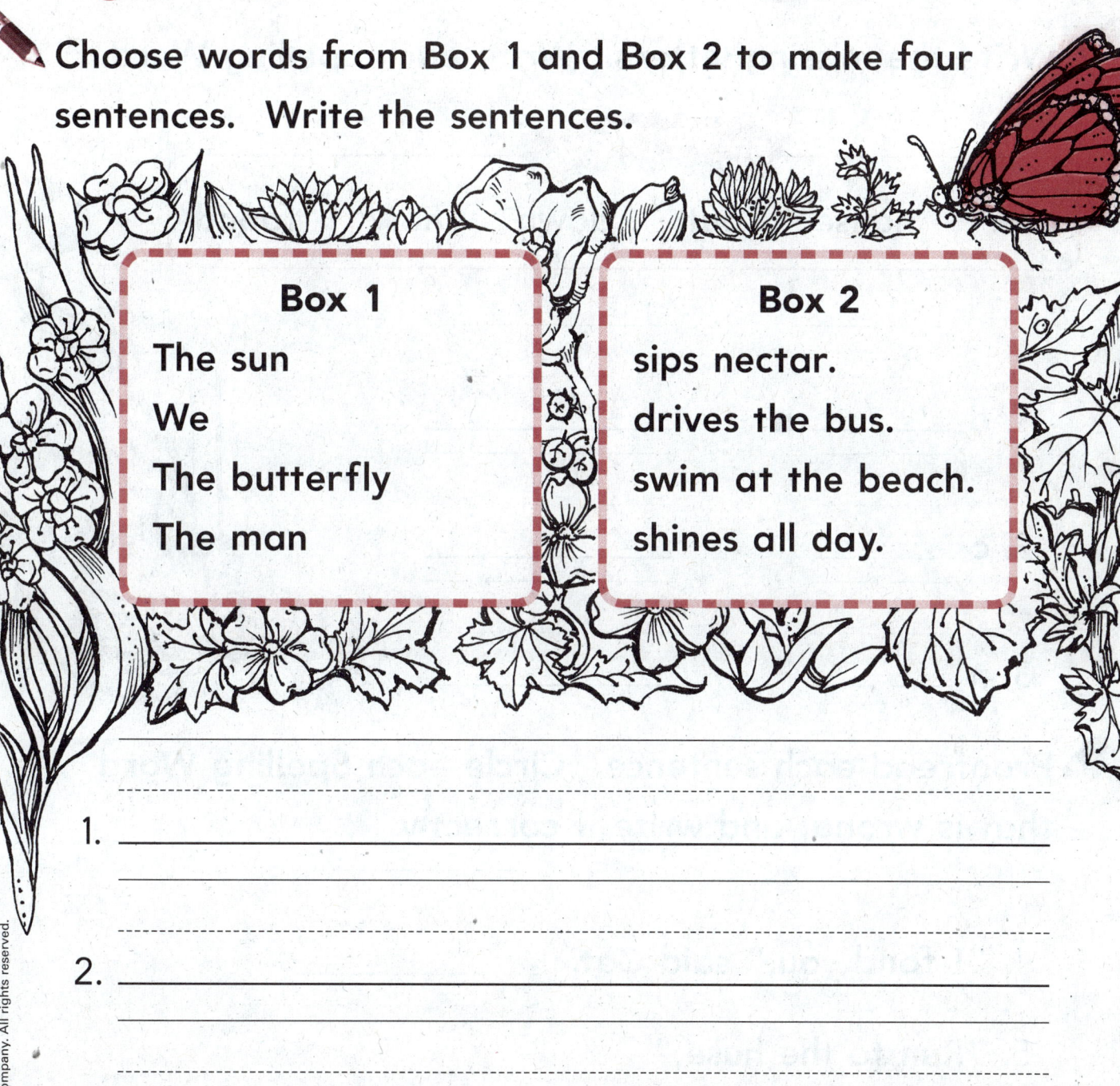

Choose words from Box 1 and Box 2 to make four sentences. Write the sentences.

Box 1

The sun
We
The butterfly
The man

Box 2

sips nectar.
drives the bus.
swim at the beach.
shines all day.

1. _____

2. _____

3. _____

4. _____

Theme 8: **Our Earth** 177

Name _____

Spelling Spree

Week 2
Spelling The Vowel Sound in *cow*

Write the missing letters. Write each Spelling Word.

Spelling Words

| cow | house | out | down | now | found |

1. d ___ ___ n _____

2. c ___ ___ _____

3. n ___ ___ _____

Proofread each sentence. Circle each Spelling Word that is wrong, and write it correctly.

4. "I fond you," said Cat. _____

5. "Run to the huse," said Mouse. _____

6. "Come owt!" said Cat. _____

178 Theme 8: **Our Earth**

Name _____

Week 2

Writing Informational Paragraph

Write About a Topic

Plan your paragraph.

1. What will you write about?

2. What is the main idea?

3. Write two sentences to explain your main idea.

Theme 8: **Our Earth** 179

A Good Move

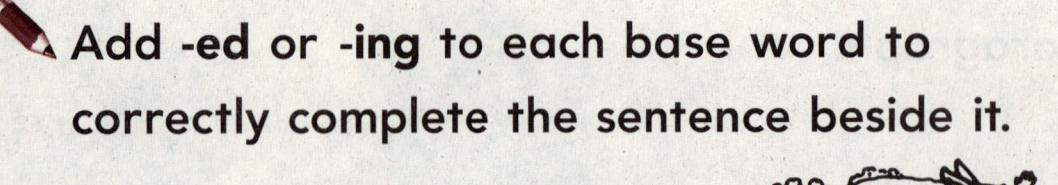

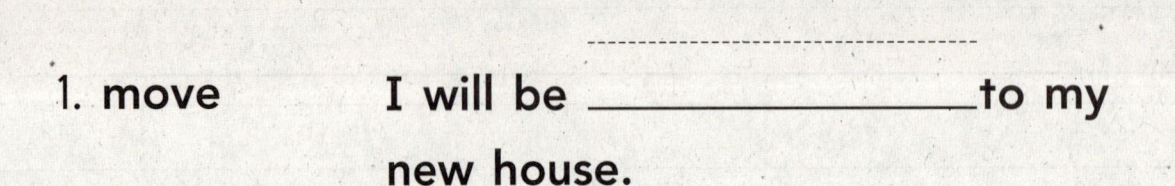

Add **-ed** or **-ing** to each base word to correctly complete the sentence beside it.

1. move — I will be _____ to my new house.

2. come — My friend will be _____ to see me.

3. stop — His car _____ in front of my house.

4. wave — I _____ to my friend.

Week 3
High-Frequency Words

Name _____

Words to Know

Write a word from the box to complete each sentence.

Word Bank

| put | work | carry | were | person |

1. We _____ going to see Mr. Wheat.

2. He is a kind _____ who bakes bread.

3. Mr. Wheat does a lot of _____.

4. I saw him _____ butter on a loaf.

5. "You can _____ this home," he said.

Theme 8: **Our Earth** 181

Name _____

Week 3

High-Frequency Words

Words to Know

Read the story. Draw a picture to go with it.

A kind girl saw a person with four big bags of butter, eggs, and other foods. "Can I help you carry those bags?" asked the girl.

"Why, thank you," said Mrs. Lee. "These bags were about to fall."

"This will work. Put two bags in my arms," said the girl.

182 Theme 8: **Our Earth**

Name _____

Week 3
Story Vocabulary *Johnny Appleseed*

Gramp's Stories

Circle and write the word that completes each sentence.

1. Many _____ ago, Gramps lived on a ranch.

    parts   years

2. As a young boy, he cleaned his clothes in the _____ .

    river   nest

3. He helped mash apples to make _____ .

    work   cider

4. He helped make _____ for meals.

    bread   stories

Theme 8: **Our Earth**   183

Name _____

Week 3

Comprehension Check
Johnny Appleseed

Apples, Apples, Apples

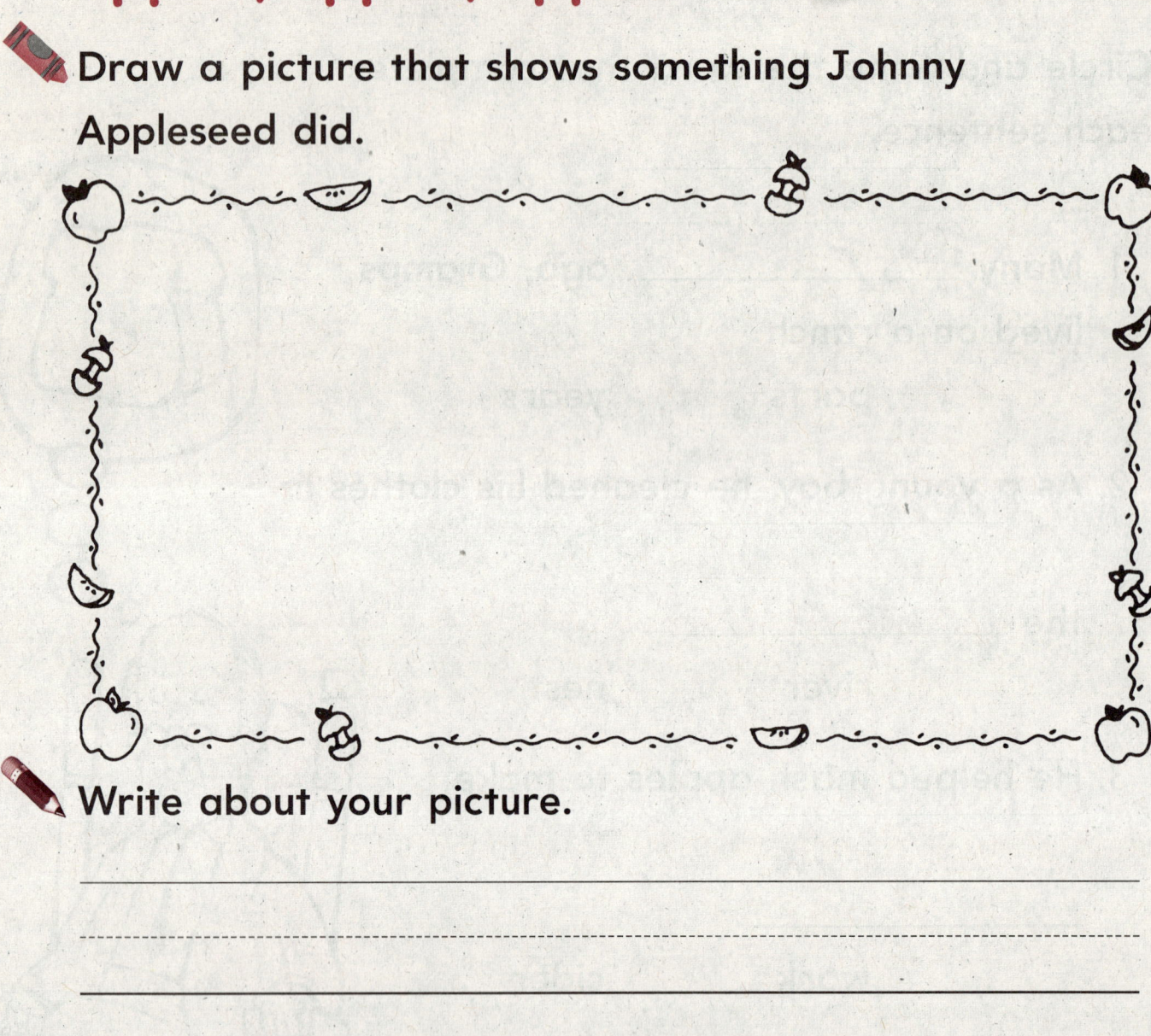

Draw a picture that shows something Johnny Appleseed did.

Write about your picture.

_____
_____
_____
_____
_____
_____

184 Theme 8: **Our Earth**

Name _____

Week 3

Comprehension Drawing Conclusions

A New Pet

Read the story and complete the chart.

    Dave and Deb wanted a pet. Deb wanted a dog. Dave wanted a cat. One day they heard a bark coming from inside the house.

Conclusion:
_____
_____
_____

Story Clues:
_____
_____
_____
_____

What You Know:
_____
_____
_____
_____

Theme 8: **Our Earth** 185

Name _____

Words with -ed or -ing

Write the correct Spelling Word under each clue.

1. looking for something

2. made something full

3. not being awake

4. did not catch

5. came down to the ground

6. talking about something

Week 3

Spelling Words That End with -ed or -ing

Spelling Words

landed
checking
telling
missed
filled
sleeping

186 Theme 8: **Our Earth**

Name _____

Week 3

Vocabulary Homophones

Sounds the Same

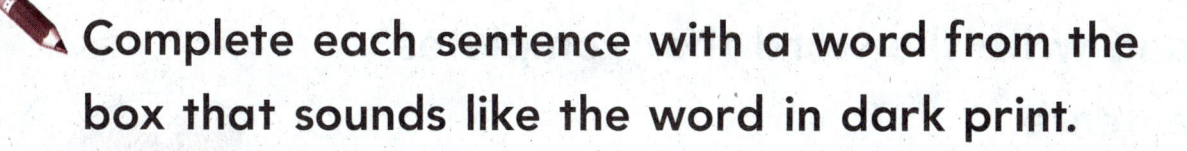

Complete each sentence with a word from the box that sounds like the word in dark print.

Word Bank			
new	for	to	eight

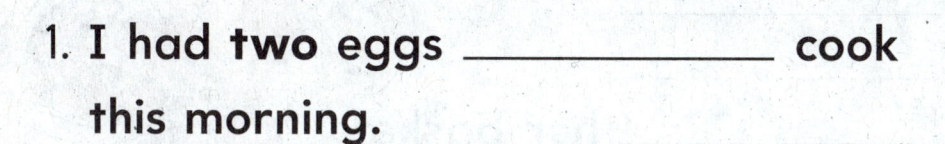

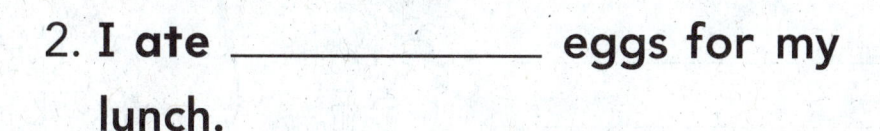

1. I had **two** eggs _____ cook this morning.

2. I **ate** _____ eggs for my lunch.

3. I had **four** eggs _____ a snack.

4. That's when I **knew** it was time to find a _____ food!

Theme 8: Our Earth   187

Name _____

Week 3

Grammar Action Words with -ed

Filled It, Spilled It!

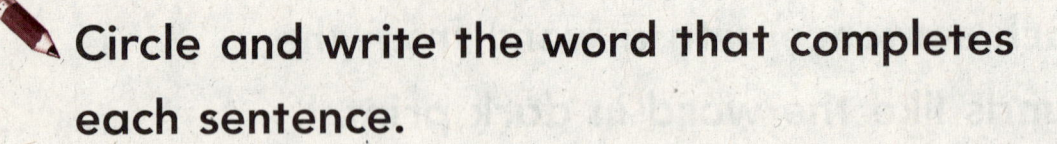

✏️ Circle and write the word that completes each sentence.

1. Liz _____ a lot.

   picked   pick

2. She _____ her basket.

   filled   fill

3. Then she _____.

   slipping   slipped

4. So Liz _____ soup.

   cook   cooked

188 Theme 8: **Our Earth**

Name _____

Week 3

Spelling Words That End with *-ed* or *-ing*

Spelling Spree

Write three Spelling Words that end with **-ed**.

1. _____
2. _____
3. _____

Spelling Words

landed
checking
telling
missed
filled
sleeping

Proofread each sentence. Circle each Spelling Word that is wrong, and write it correctly.

4. Mom was cheking the bag.   _____

5. She was tellng me to help.   _____

6. I was slepin!   _____

Theme 8: **Our Earth**   189

Name _____

Week 3

Writing Writing with Action Words

Writing Clearly

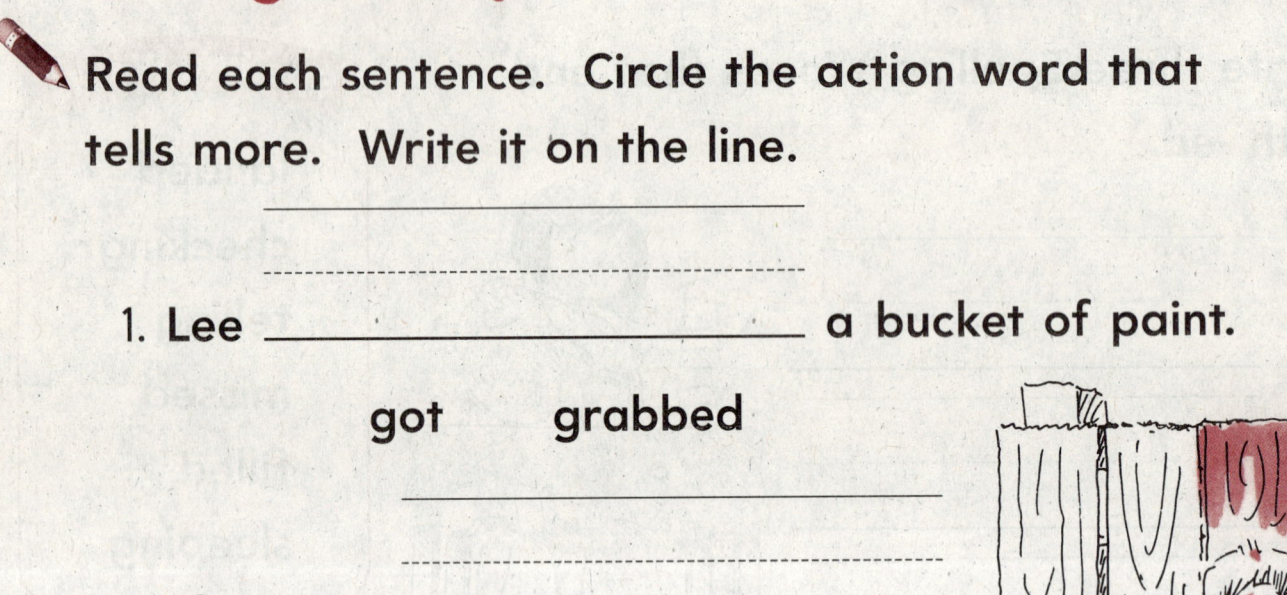

Read each sentence. Circle the action word that tells more. Write it on the line.

1. Lee _____ a bucket of paint.

   got   grabbed

2. The paint _____.

   slipped   fell

3. It _____ on Lee's cat.

   went   dripped

4. It _____ on Lee's pants.

   got   sprayed

5. Paint _____ everywhere!

   splashed   was

190 Theme 8: Our Earth

Name _____

Our Earth

Taking Tests

Choosing the Best Answer

Now use what you have learned about taking tests. Answer these questions about the story **Johnny Appleseed**. Look back at the story if you need to. This practice will help you when you take this kind of test.

Read each question. Fill in the circle next to the best answer.

1. Why did Johnny Appleseed want to plant apple seeds?
   ○ He wanted to eat apples.
   ○ He liked planting seeds.
   ○ He wanted to make the West a nice place to live.

2. What kind of hat did Johnny Appleseed wear?
   ○ A cooking pot
   ○ A cap
   ○ A rag

Theme 8: **Our Earth**   191

Name _____

Choosing the Best Answer

continued

3 What did Johnny do when it snowed?
   ○ He stopped.
   ○ He made snowshoes.
   ○ He started running.

4 Where did Johnny plant the first apple seed?
   ○ By an apple tree
   ○ On a hill
   ○ By a river

5 How did Johnny feel about wild animals?
   ○ He was afraid of wild animals.
   ○ He was not afraid of wild animals.
   ○ He did not like wild animals.

6 Where did Johnny sleep?
   ○ On a bed
   ○ In a house
   ○ Under the stars

Name _____

Our Earth:
Theme 8 Wrap-Up
Spelling Review

Spelling Review

Add or take off an ending to make each word into a Spelling Word from the box. Write the Spelling Word.

Spelling Words

frog
trees
out
now
filled
checking

1. tree _____

2. fill _____

3. check _____

4. frogs _____

Write the two Spelling Words that have the vowel sound you hear in **owl**.

5. _____

6. _____

Theme 8: **Our Earth**   193

**Our Earth:
Theme 8 Wrap-Up**

Spelling Review

Name _____

Spelling Spree

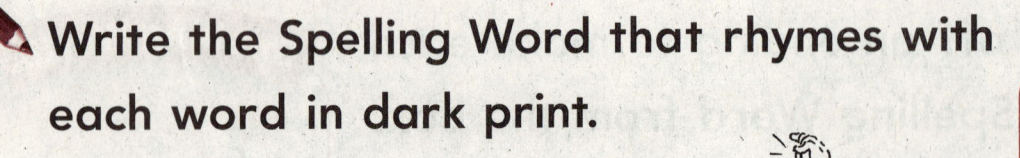

Write the Spelling Word that rhymes with each word in dark print.

Spelling Words
- frog
- trees
- out
- now
- sleeping
- found

1. You can hear her **shout**, _____

   "My tooth fell _____!"

2. The clock is **beeping**, _____

   but he is still _____.

3. That is a hungry **cow**. _____

   We will feed her _____.

Proofread each sentence. Circle each Spelling Word that is wrong, and write it correctly.

4. Treas can be homes for animals. _____

5. Birds can be fownd in the tops. _____

6. A frogg can live there, too! _____

194   Theme 8: Our Earth

Name _____

Week 1
Phonics Sounds for y

Lucky Duck

Circle the words that have the **y** sound you hear in **try**. Underline the words that have the **y** sound you hear in **sunny**. Write the words.

Dan lives in the city by a big pond. Dan likes bright days when the sky is blue. When a day is rainy, that's all right, too!

try

1. _____

2. _____

sunny

3. _____

4. _____

Theme 9: **Special Friends** 195

Name _____

Week 1

Phonics Sounds for *y*

Try These

✏️ Write the words from the box that name each picture.

> a sunny sky   my lucky penny   a muddy spy
> a flying kitty   a shy bunny

1. _____

2. _____

3. _____

4. _____

5. _____

196   Theme 9: **Special Friends**

Name _____

Words to Know

Week 1
High-Frequency Words

Circle and write the correct word to complete each sentence.

1. We love to be around the _____.

   though   ocean   else

2. We _____ in the waves.

   ever   dance   though

3. We _____ a box of snacks.

   ocean   around   open

4. Even though it's cool, it's the best day _____!

   ever   dance   talk

Theme 9: **Special Friends**   197

Name _____

Week 1
High-Frequency Words

Words to Know

Write the correct word from the box for each clue.

Word Bank

ever	talk	dance	ocean
though	else	around	open

1. Ask someone ___.

2. Means "to speak"

3. Sounds like **never**

4. Means "the sea"

5. Sounds like **go**

6. Not closed

7. We sing and ___.

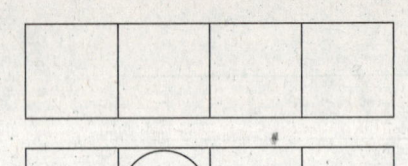

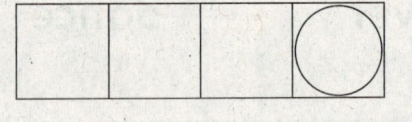

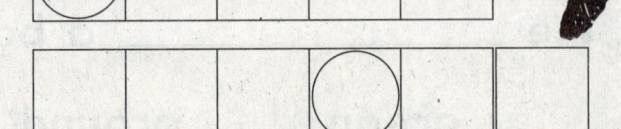

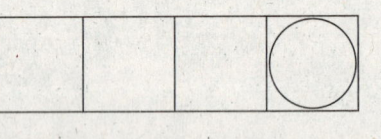

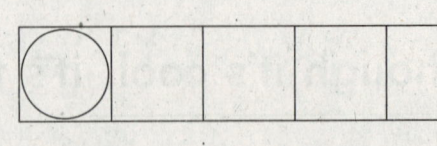

Write the letter from each circle.

___ ___ ___ ___ ___ ___ ___

198 Theme 9: **Special Friends**

Week 1

Story Vocabulary When I Am Old with You

Name _____

Remember When

Read the story, and draw a picture to go with it.

I don't grow tired of playing "Remember When" with Grandaddy. We get all of his old cards out of his cedar chest. He has to imagine the picture in his mind as I tell him what I see. Grandaddy loves the one with the canoe in the big field of flowers.

Name _____

Week 1

Comprehension Check
When I Am Old with You

What Did They Do?

List five things that the child and Grandaddy will do when they are old.

1. _____

2. _____

3. _____

4. _____

5. _____

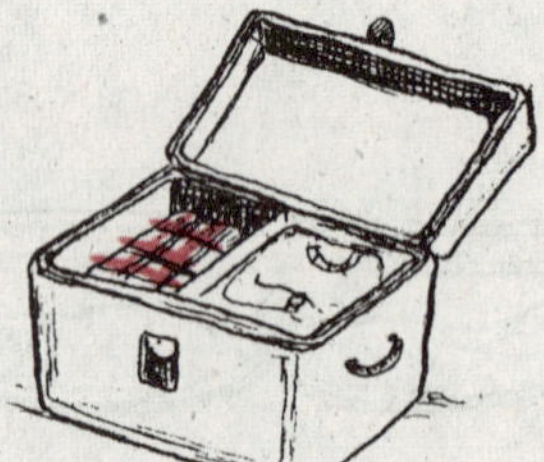

Theme 9: **Special Friends**

Name _____

At the Pond

Look at this picture. Write about two silly things you see.

1. _____

2. _____

Theme 9: **Special Friends** 201

Name _____

Week 1

Spelling The Long *i* Sound Spelled *y*

The Long *i* Sound Spelled *y*

Write a word from the box to complete each sentence.

Word Bank

| by | my | fly | try | cry | why |

1. Little Bird stood _____ Mother.

2. He was so sad he was about to _____.

3. "I don't think _____ wings work," he said.

4. "I want to _____ up in the sky!" he said.

5. "I don't see _____ not," said Mother.

6. "You can do it if you _____."

202 Theme 9: **Special Friends**

Week 1

Vocabulary Sensory Words

Name _____

Sense It

Write the word pair that describes each picture.

> soft, fuzzy   loud, jazzy
> bright, hot   crispy, crunchy

1.  _____ sun

2.  _____ toast

3.  _____ cat

4.  _____ band

Theme 9: **Special Friends** 203

Name _____

Week 1

Grammar *Is* and *Are*

Go, Jane, Go!

✏ Write **is** or **are** to complete each sentence.

is   are

1. It _____ the day of the Fun Run.

2. Beth and Jane _____ in the race.

3. Jane _____ very fast.

4. The race _____ on!

5. You _____ going to win, Jane!

204 Theme 9: **Special Friends**

Name _____

Week 1

Spelling The Long *i* Sound Spelled *y*

Spelling Spree

✏️ Circle and write the hidden Spelling Words.

Spelling Words

| by | my | fly | try | cry | why |

1. scryth _____

2. scafly _____

3. smylie _____

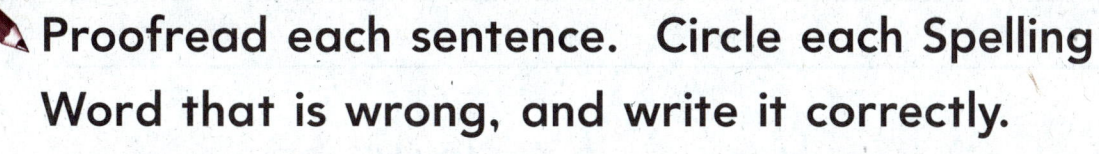

✏️ Proofread each sentence. Circle each Spelling Word that is wrong, and write it correctly.

4. Whie are you crying? _____

5. Come sit bigh me. _____

6. I will tri to help. _____

Theme 9: **Special Friends** 205

Name _____

Week 1

Writing Response to Literature

Story Response

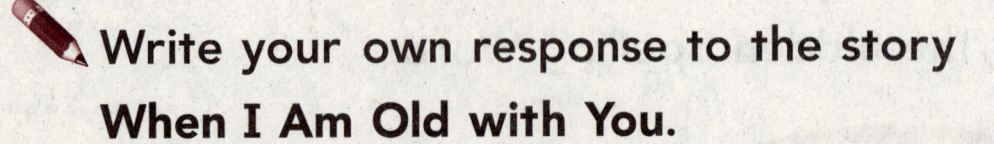

✏️ Write your own response to the story **When I Am Old with You.**

Title: _____

What did you think of the story?
_____
_____
_____

Would you recommend it to a friend? Why?
_____
_____
_____

206 Theme 9: **Special Friends**

Reading-Writing Workshop

Revising Your Friendly Letter

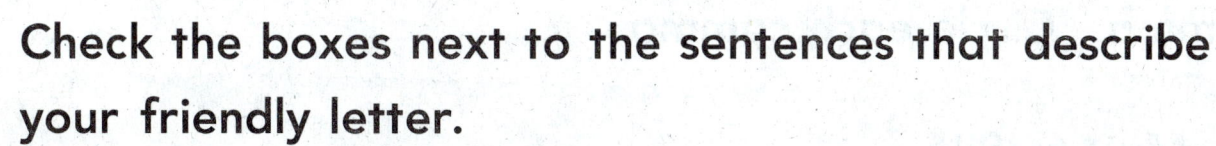

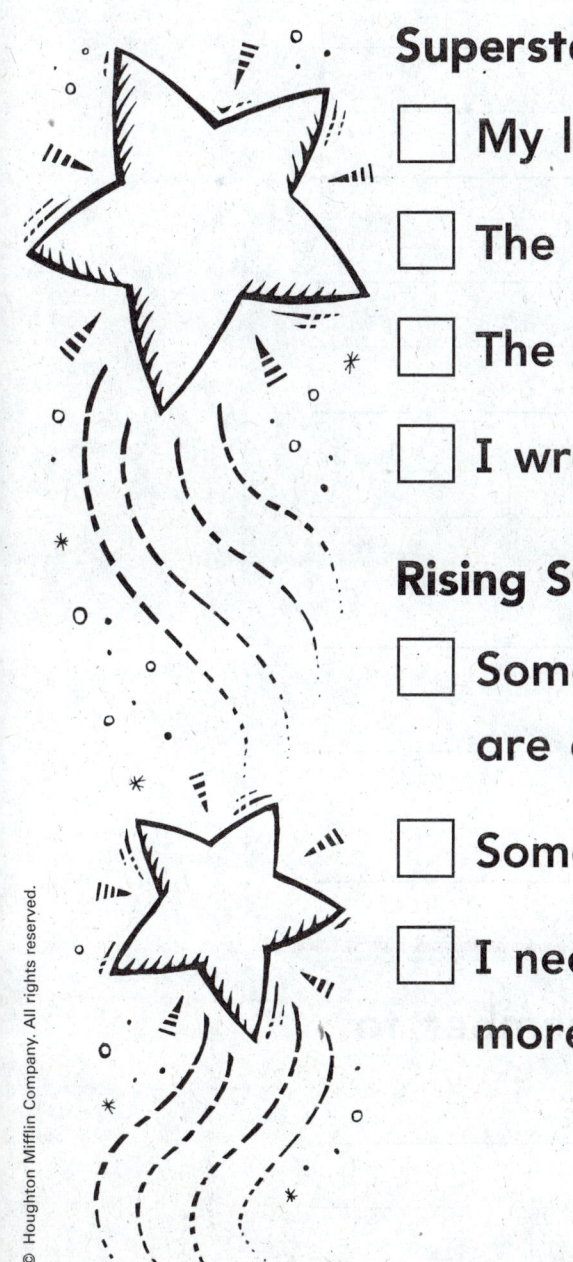

Revising Your Friendly Letter

Check the boxes next to the sentences that describe your friendly letter.

Superstar

☐ My letter has all five parts in it.

☐ The parts of my letter are complete.

☐ The body of my letter makes sense.

☐ I wrote interesting details in my letter.

Rising Star

☐ Some parts of my letter are missing or are out of order.

☐ Some parts are not complete.

☐ I need more details to make my letter more interesting.

Theme 9: **Special Friends**

Name _____

Reading-Writing Workshop

Friendly Letter Using Commas in Dates

What's Missing?

✏️ Write each date correctly by adding a comma. Circle each comma.

1. May 6 1945

2. August 9 2000

3. February 1 1989

4. September 23 2002

✏️ Write today's date correctly. Remember to write the year.

208   Theme 9: **Special Friends**

Name _____

Week 2

Phonics Base Words and Endings *-es, -ies*

Add It On

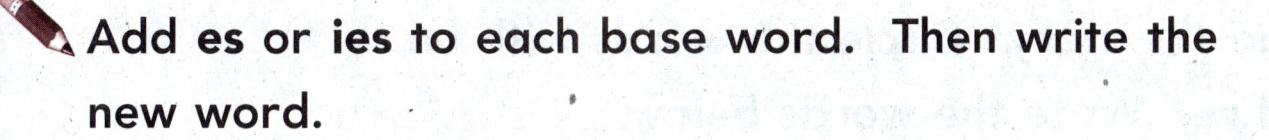

Add **es** or **ies** to each base word. Then write the new word.

1. dish

2. hatch

3. bunny

4. fox

5. glass

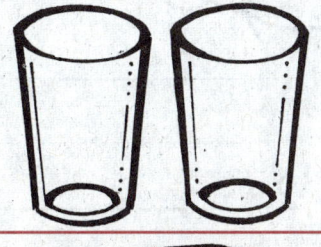

6. peach

Theme 9: **Special Friends** 209

Name _____

Week 2

Phonics Prefixes *un-*, *re-*

Is it *un* or *re*?

Read the story. Circle the words with **un** and **re**. Write the words below.

I think I forgot to pack my socks! Now I have to unpack my bag to check. First, I must unsnap it! Then I will have to refill it. I don't mind redoing it!

1. _____ 2. _____

3. _____ 4. _____

210   Theme 9: **Special Friends**

Name _____

Words to Know

Write the correct word from the box for each clue.

Word Bank

| after | before | buy | pretty |
| school | done | off | wash |

1. Means "complete"
   _____

2. Not before
   _____

3. Means "nice to look at"
   _____

4. Means "to pay for"
   _____

5. It's a place to learn.
   _____

6. Means "to clean"
   _____

7. Not on
   _____

8. Not after
   _____

Theme 9: **Special Friends** 211

Name _____

Week 2

High-Frequency Words

Words to Know

Read each sentence. Draw a picture to go with it.

After school today, my dad is taking me to buy the pretty dress we saw in the shop.

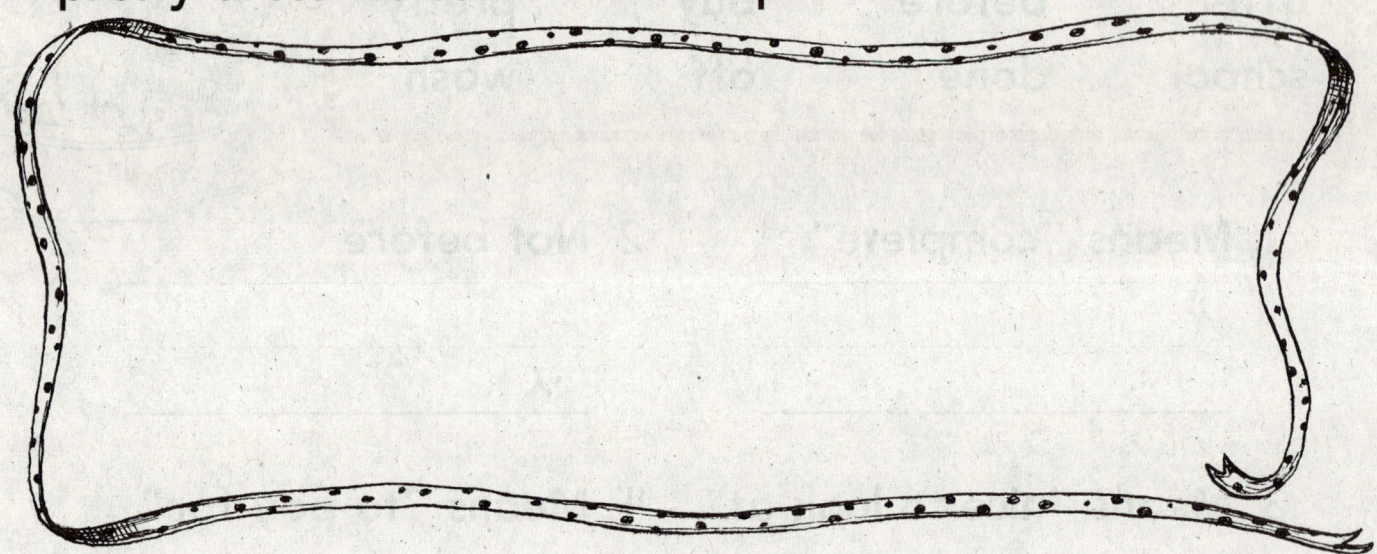

When I am done making cookies, I will wash off the table before lunch.

212   Theme 9: **Special Friends**

Name _____

Week 2

Story Vocabulary *The New Friend*

Come to a Party!

Read the invitation.

Come to a Birthday Party!

Place: Seventh City Soccer Club

When: May 7, 2002

We'll have lots of cookies and cake to fill your empty tummy! This will be the best party in years!

Draw what you would bring to this party.

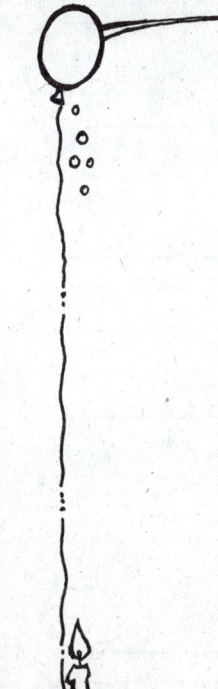

Theme 9: **Special Friends** 213

Name _____

Week 2

Comprehension Check *The New Friend*

What Happened?

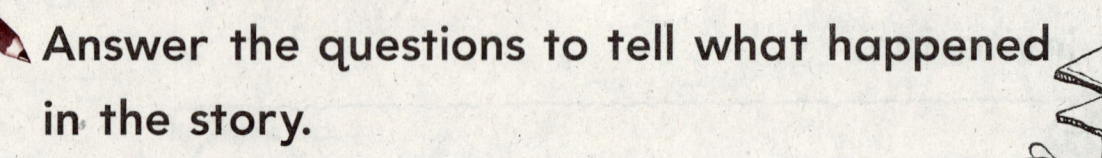

Answer the questions to tell what happened in the story.

1. Who moved into the empty house?
   _____
   _____
   _____

2. Where was Makoto from?
   _____
   _____

3. What did all the boys like to do?
   _____
   _____
   _____

4. What made the boys glad?
   _____
   _____
   _____

Theme 9: **Special Friends**

Name _____

Week 2
Comprehension Story Structure

Map Out the Story

Think about the story **Lost!** Complete the story map.

Characters: _____
_____

Setting: _____
_____

Problem: _____
_____
_____

Solution: _____
_____
_____

Theme 9: **Special Friends**

Name _____

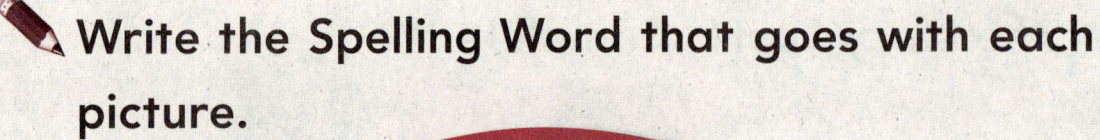

Week 2

Spelling Adding *-es* to Naming Words

Adding *es* to Naming Words

Write the Spelling Word that goes with each picture.

Spelling Words

| dishes | dresses | boxes |
| beaches | wishes | kisses |

1. _____

2. _____

3. _____

4. _____

Write the two Spelling Words that are left.

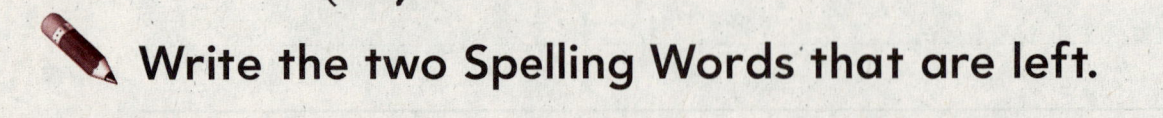

5. _____   6. _____

216 Theme 9: **Special Friends**

Week 2

Vocabulary Synonyms

Name _____

Another Word for It

Read each word in dark print. Write a word from the box that has the same meaning.

Word Bank

big   little   clean   picture   friend   glad

1. **buddy**
   _____
   _____

2. **huge**
   _____
   _____

3. **happy**
   _____
   _____

4. **scrub**
   _____
   _____

5. **small**
   _____
   _____

6. **drawing**
   _____
   _____

Theme 9: **Special Friends**   217

Name _____

Week 2

Grammar *Was* and *Were*

Using *Was* and *Were*

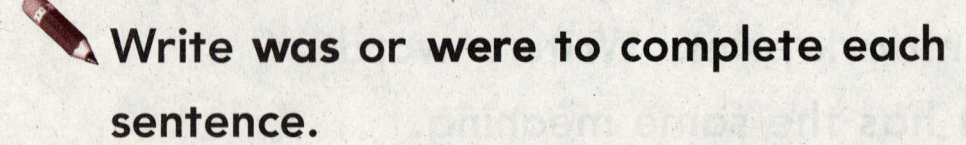

Write **was** or **were** to complete each sentence.

1. I _____ meeting my friends.

2. We _____ going to play catch.

3. Where _____ my two friends?

4. One friend _____ home sick.

5. Two of us _____ playing on our own.

218 Theme 9: **Special Friends**

Name _____

Spelling Spree

Week 2

Spelling Adding *-es* to Naming Words

Write the two Spelling Words that rhyme.

Spelling Words

| dishes | dresses | boxes |
| beaches | wishes | kisses |

1. _____ 2. _____

Proofread each sentence. Circle the Spelling Word that is wrong, and write it correctly.

3. Fred dreses in trunks. _____

4. He gets boxs. _____

5. He kissis Mom. _____

6. Fred's off to the beashes. _____

Theme 9: **Special Friends**   219

Week 2

Writing Complete Sentences

Name _____

Finish Them Up

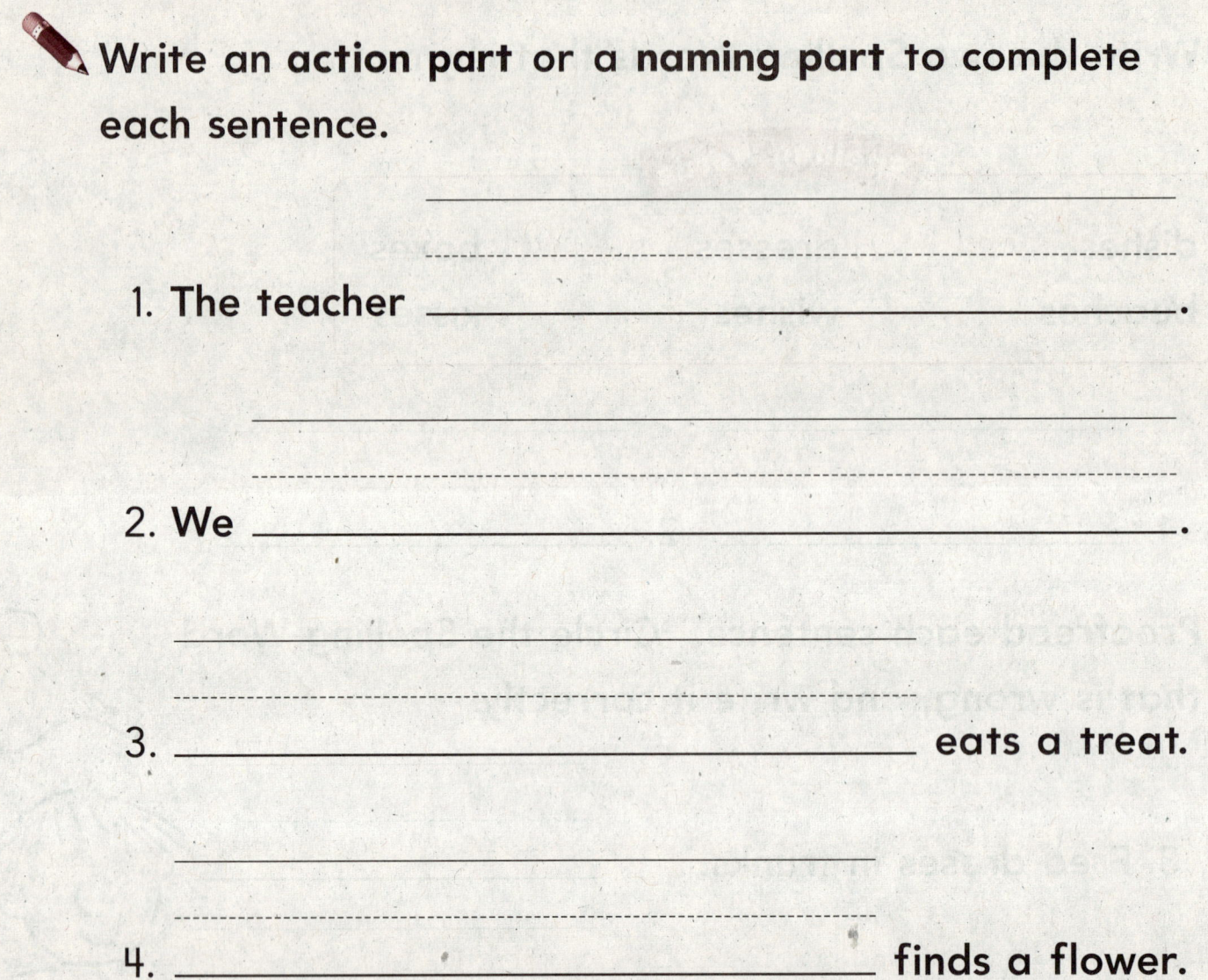

Write an **action part** or a **naming part** to complete each sentence.

1. The teacher _____.

2. We _____.

3. _____ eats a treat.

4. _____ finds a flower.

220 Theme 9: **Special Friends**

Name _____

Week 3

Phonics Vowel Pairs *oi, oy; aw, au*

Rhyming Words

Write a rhyming word for each word.

1. **joy**
   _____
   _____
   _____

2. **vault**
   _____
   _____
   _____

3. **jaw**
   _____
   _____
   _____

4. **dawn**
   _____
   _____
   _____

5. **oil**
   _____
   _____
   _____

6. **paw**
   _____
   _____
   _____

Theme 9: **Special Friends**

Name _____

Week 3

Phonics Vowel Pairs *oi*, *oy*; *aw*, *au*

A New Home for Duck

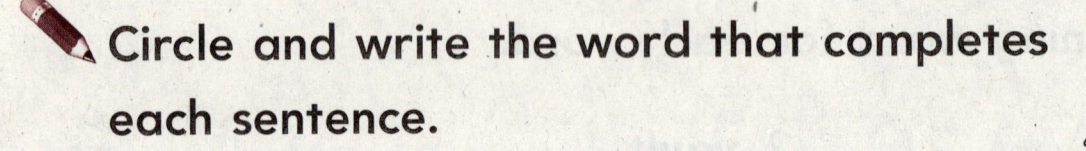

✏️ Circle and write the word that completes each sentence.

1. Fox _____ Duck packing up.

   soil   sauce   saw

2. She _____ Duck to help.

   joined   jaw   boiled

3. The friends _____ the big things in a van.

   taught   hauled   clawed

4. "Thanks!" said Duck with _____ .

   jaw   joy   join

222 Theme 9: **Special Friends**

Week 3

Phonics Suffixes -ful, -ly, -y

Name _____

Words with ful, ly, y

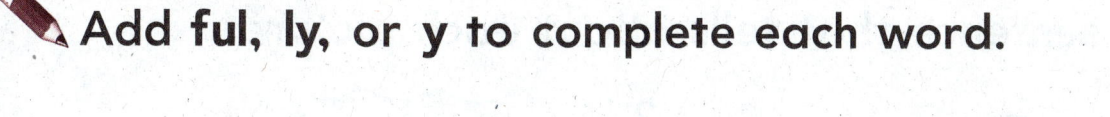

Add **ful**, **ly**, or **y** to complete each word.

1. help _____
2. use _____
3. quick _____
4. loud _____
5. squeak _____
6. luck _____

Write a word that ends with **ful** or **y** to complete the sentence.

7. I am _____ to have you for a friend.

Theme 9: **Special Friends** 223

Week 3

High-Frequency Words

Name _____

Words to Know

✏️ Circle the sentence that tells about each picture.

1.

We all went together.

I only had two cookies.

2.

The garden is full of flowers.

We had enough time to swim.

3.

We played at the edge of the water.

The baby can't swim yet.

4.

We watched the fishing boats come in.

That is a sharp edge!

224 Theme 9: **Special Friends**

Name _____

Week 3

High-Frequency Words

Words to Know

Read the story. Draw a picture to go with it.

    We worked together in the garden. The baby watched us work. I used a garden tool with sharp points. We had only a small garden, so we had enough flower seeds to plant. We put pretty flowers around the edge of our garden.

Theme 9: **Special Friends**   225

Week 3
Story Vocabulary

Name _____

Our Chickens

Write words from the box to complete the story.

Word Bank

gathered   built   taught   danger   feathers

I _____ my chickens a henhouse. Then I _____ them to sleep in it. When they expected to be fed, they _____ at the door. They ate grit for their gizzards. Then they fluffed their _____.

When they saw the vacuum cleaner, they squawked, "Awwk!" It was their _____ cry.

226   Theme 9: **Special Friends**

Name _____

Week 3

Comprehension Check *The Surprise Family*

Alike and Different

What was so surprising about the hen's family? Write and draw your answer.

Theme 9: **Special Friends** 227

Week 3

Comprehension Compare and Contrast

Name _____

Sue and Sam

✏️ Read the story, and answer the questions.

Sue and Sam are twins.
Sam is tall, and Sue is not.
Sue loves baseball.
Sam sings and plays in a jazz band.
Both Sue and Sam like to read and write.

How are Sue and Sam alike?
_____
_____
_____

How are Sue and Sam different?
_____
_____
_____

228   Theme 9: **Special Friends**

Name _____

The Vowel Sound in *coin*

Week 3
Spelling The Vowel Sound in *coin*

Use the letter for each shape to write two Spelling Words.

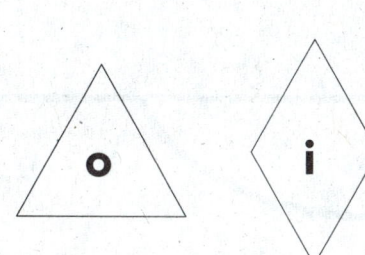

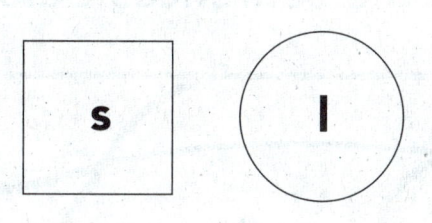

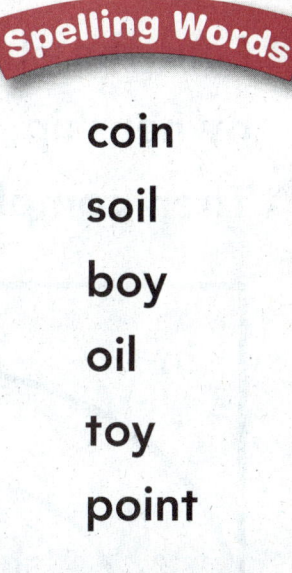

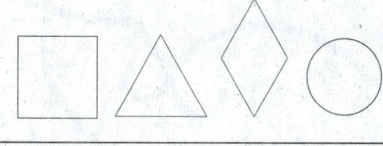

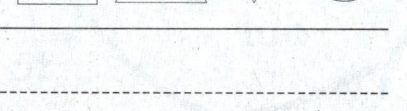

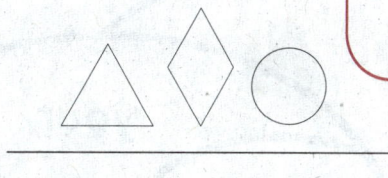

Spelling Words

- coin
- soil
- boy
- oil
- toy
- point

1. _____
2. _____

Write the Spelling Word that goes with each picture.

3. _____

4. _____

5. _____

6. _____

Theme 9: **Special Friends**   229

Name _____

Week 3

Vocabulary Possessive Pronouns

Puzzle Fun

🖍️ Find the shapes with words that show ownership. Color then orange.

✏️ Then complete the sentences below.

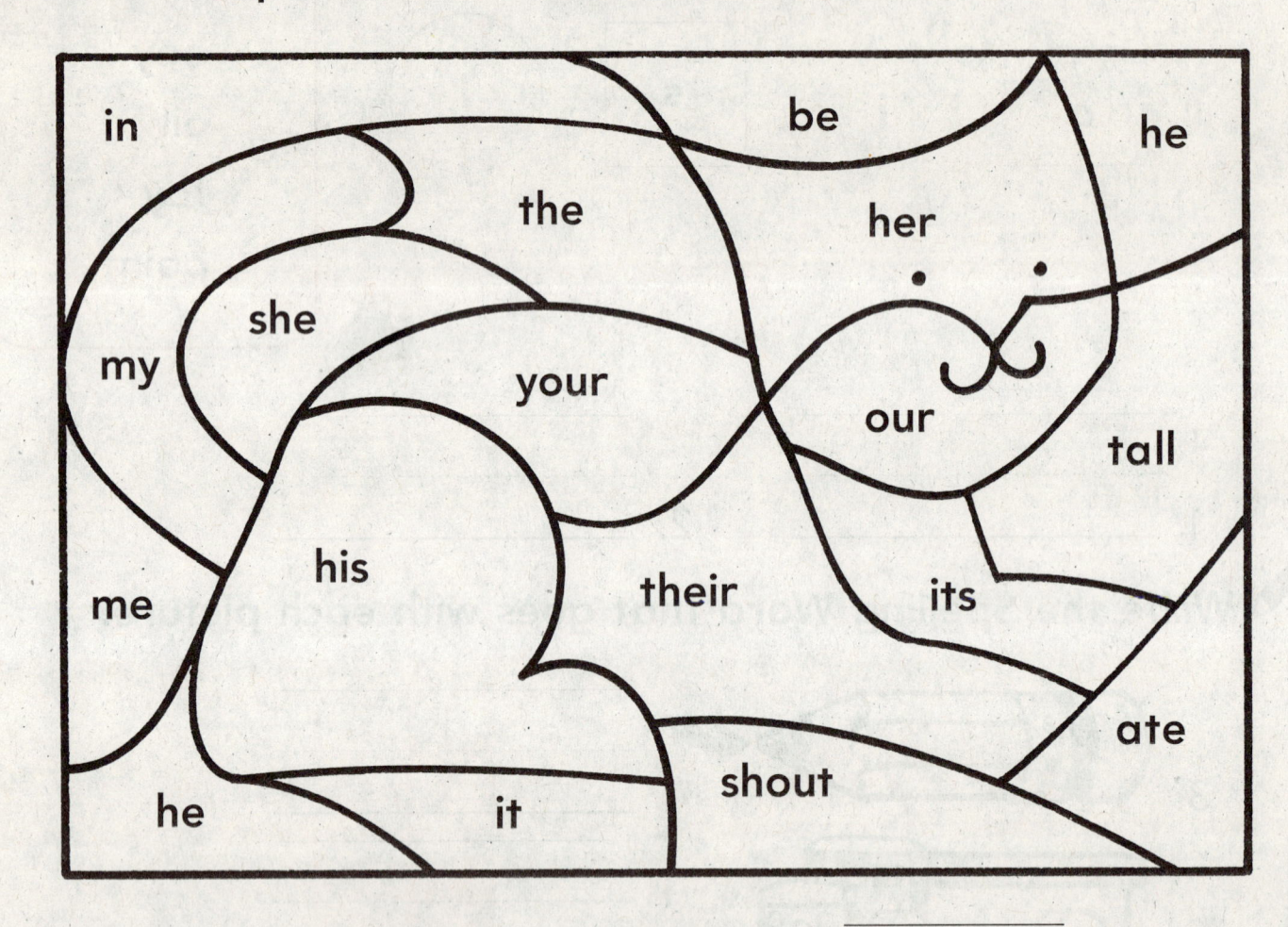

(puzzle containing words: in, be, he, the, her, she, my, your, our, tall, his, their, its, me, ate, shout, he, it)

1. If this pet belongs to a girl, it is _____ pet.

2. If this pet belongs to a boy, it is _____ pet.

230   Theme 9: **Special Friends**

Name _____

Color, Number, Size, Shape

Week 3

Grammar Describing What We See

Read the clues in ( ). Then write a describing word to complete each sentence.
Draw a picture to go with your description.

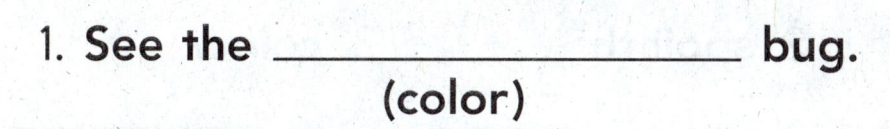

1. See the _____ bug.
   (color)

2. It is very _____!
   (size)

3. It has a _____ face.
   (shape)

4. It has _____ legs.
   (number)

Theme 9: **Special Friends** 231

Name _____

Week 3

Spelling The Vowel Sound in *coin*

Spelling Spree

✏️ Circle and write the hidden Spelling Words.

Spelling Words

| coin | soil | boy | oil | toy | point |

1. froboil

2. spointh

3. coinex

✏️ Proofread each sentence. Circle each Spelling Word that is wrong, and write it correctly.

4. What does this boi have?

5. It is a toye.

6. It digs up soyl.

232 Theme 9: **Special Friends**

Name _____

Week 3

Writing Writing a Comparison

Compare Them!

Look at the pictures, and answer the questions.

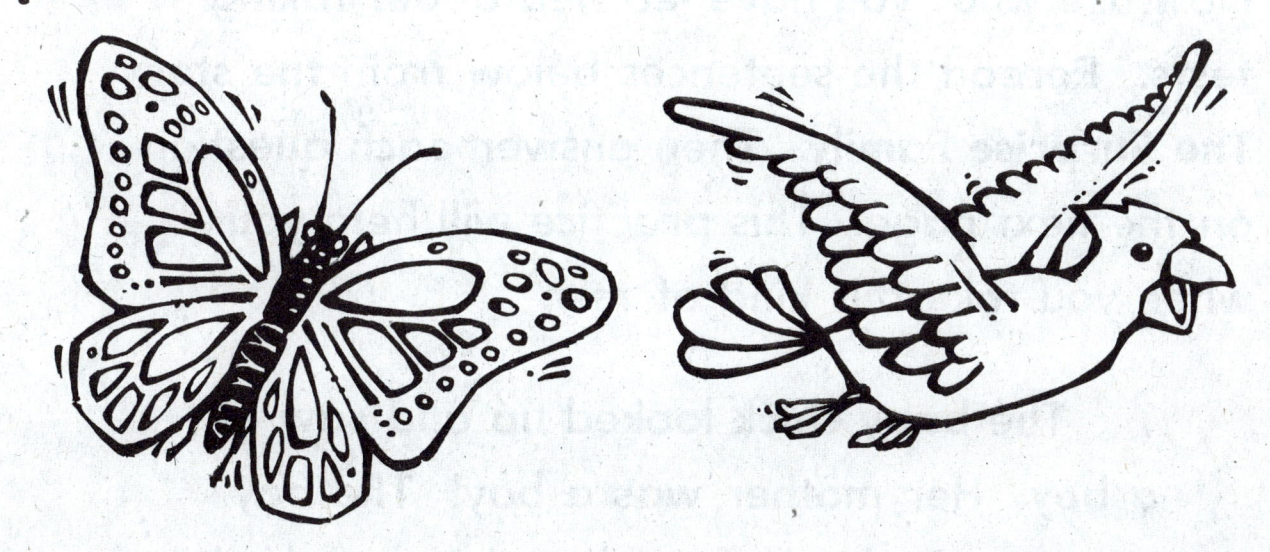

1. How are they alike?
   _____
   _____
   _____
   _____

2. How are they different?
   _____
   _____
   _____
   _____

Theme 9: **Special Friends** 233

Name _____

Special Friends

Taking Tests

Writing an Answer to a Question

Now use what you have learned about taking tests. Reread the sentences below from the story **The Surprise Family**. Then answer each question on the next page. This practice will help you when you take this kind of test.

> The baby chick looked up and saw — a boy. Her mother was a boy! The boy was not the kind of mother the chick had expected, but she loved him anyway. She followed him everywhere.
>
> The boy showed his baby chick how to find water and food and grit for her gizzard. He taught her how to hide safe inside his jacket when a hawk flew by or when the vacuum cleaner came too close.

234   Theme 9: **Special Friends**

Name _____

Writing an Answer to a Question continued

Write your answer to each question.

1 What kind of mother do you think the chick expected? Why?

_____
_____
_____
_____
_____

2 What does the boy do for the chick?

_____
_____
_____
_____
_____

Name _____

Spelling Review

**Special Friends:
Theme 9 Wrap-Up**

Spelling Review

✏️ Add **es** to each word to spell a word from the box. Write each word.

Spelling Words

cry
boxes
wishes
boy
dresses
coin

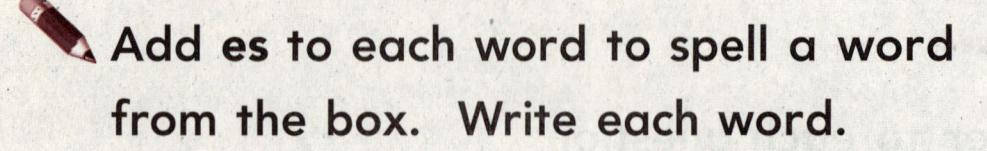

1. **dress** _____

2. **box** _____

3. **wish** _____

✏️ Write the two Spelling Words that have the vowel sound you hear in **oink**.

4. _____

5. _____

✏️ Write the Spelling Word that you have not used.

6. _____

236 Theme 9: **Special Friends**

Name _____

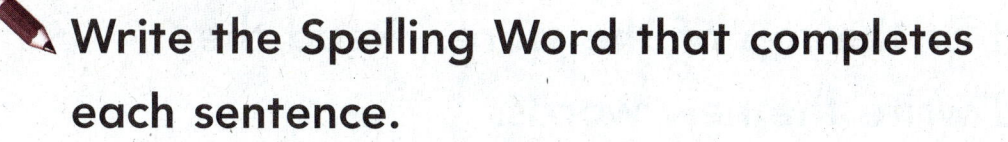

**Special Friends:
Theme 9 Wrap-Up**
Spelling Review

Spelling Spree

Write the Spelling Word that completes each sentence.

Spelling Words

point
try
boy
wishes
fly
beaches

1. The _____ plays with the baby.

2. She will _____ to get the kite.

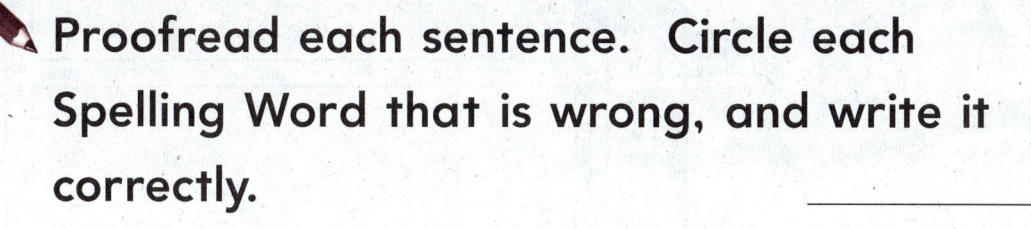

3. One crayon has a sharp _____.

Proofread each sentence. Circle each Spelling Word that is wrong, and write it correctly.

4. I would like two wishs.

5. I want to fli like a bird.

6. I want to go over beachs.

Theme 9: **Special Friends**   237

Name _____

Week 1

Phonics r-Controlled Vowels
or, ore

Word Store

Read the word at the top of the store. Read the directions, and write the new words. The starred one is done for you.

store

☆ s _ o _ r _ e

☆ Take out the **t** in **store**.
1. Change the **e** to **t**.
2. Change the **s** to **f**.
3. Take out the **t**.
4. Add **k** to the end.

1. _____
2. _____
3. _____
4. _____

Use a word from the store to complete the sentence.

I'll go to the store to _____ look _____ some more forks.

238 Theme 10: **We Can Do It!**

Name _____

Week 1
Phonics *r*-Controlled Vowels
or, ore

A Full Day

Read the story below. Write each word in dark print below the picture it names.

Jill rides a **horse**. Sam goes to the **store**. Mort plays the **horn**. Norm plants some **corn**. Others play **sports**. Nan keeps **score**. No one is bored!

1. _____

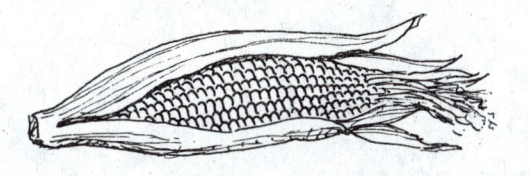

2. _____

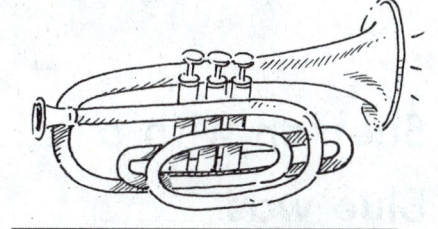

3. _____

4. _____

5. _____

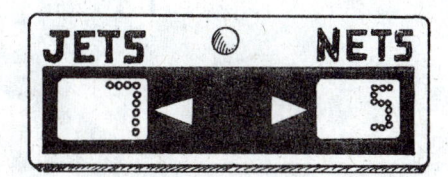

6. _____

Theme 10: **We Can Do It!** 239

Week 1

Phonics *r*-Controlled Vowels
er, ir, ur

Name _____

Jo's Home Run

Finish each sentence with a word from the Word Bank. Write each word in the correct puzzle boxes.

Word Bank

| turn | girl | burst | shirt | her | third |

Across

1. She ran with a _____ of speed.
2. Blue was _____ team's color.
3. Jo hit the ball past _____ base.

Down

4. Jo wore a blue _____ .
5. It was Jo's _____ at bat.
6. That _____ hit a home run!

240   Theme 10: We Can Do It!

Name _____

Week 1

Phonics *r*-Controlled Vowels: *er, ir, ur*

What Will Gert Wear?

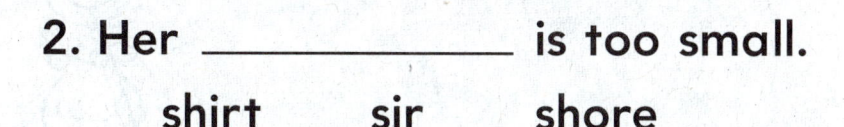

Circle and write the word that completes each sentence.

1. Gert looks at _____ three shirts.
   horse   her   fur

2. Her _____ is too small.
   shirt   sir   shore

3. This shirt is too _____ .
   day   curly   dirty

4. Here's her _____ shirt.
   stir   third   turn

5. This shirt is _____ !
   perfect   germ   bird

Theme 10: **We Can Do It!**   241

Name _____

Week 1

High-Frequency Words

Words to Know

Read each story. Draw a picture to go with it.

I can't break that candy in two. You give it a try, and I'll give it a second try. We sure can divide candy!

Jeff began to tell a joke. I began to laugh. I laughed until my head hurt!

242 Theme 10: **We Can Do It!**

Name _____

Week 1

High-Frequency Words

Words to Know

Fold a piece of paper in half to make a book.
Cut out and paste the story parts on the pages in order.
Write your own ending on the last page.

A Better Idea

Buzz and Fuzz found a log.

"Let's divide it with an ax," said Buzz. "I'm sure that will work."

"We have these big teeth!" said Fuzz. "We can chew the log in two!"

Buzz laughed, too. "Sure!" he said.

They hit the log. It didn't break. They tried a second time. Buzz shook his head. Fuzz began to laugh.

Theme 10: **We Can Do It!** 243

Week 1

Story Vocabulary *Two Greedy Bears*

Name _____

No More Arguing

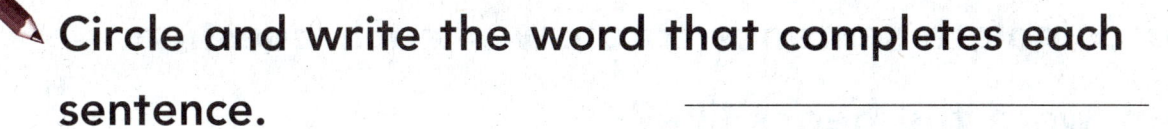

Circle and write the word that completes each sentence.

1. One piece of cake was _____ .

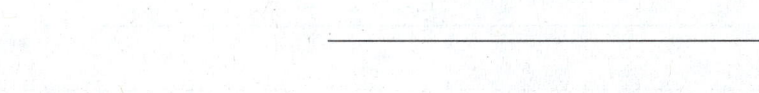

   larger   appetite

2. The pieces aren't _____ .

   journey   equal

3. Bo and Mo _____ about it.

   thirstier   argued

4. "I'm _____ than you are," said Bo.

   hungrier   arguing

5. Bo got a _____ stomachache!

   thirstier   bigger

Theme 10: **We Can Do It!**   245

Name _____

Two Greedy Bears

Write a complete sentence to answer each question.

1. What were the bears like?

2. What was the fox like?

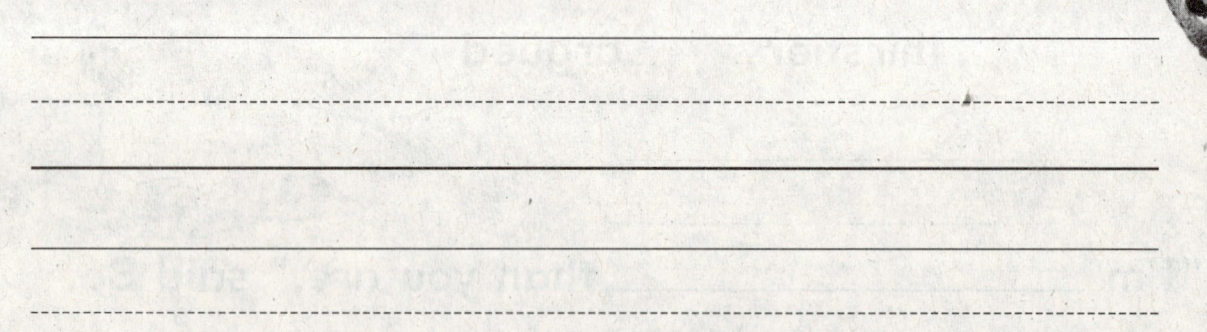

Week 1

Comprehension Check Two Greedy Bears

246 Theme 10: **We Can Do It!**

Week 1

Comprehension Making Predictions

Name _____

What Happens Next?

Read the sentences. Draw what happens next.

1. A dog is sleeping under a tree. A bag of food is next to him. A sneaky fox creeps up. What happens next?

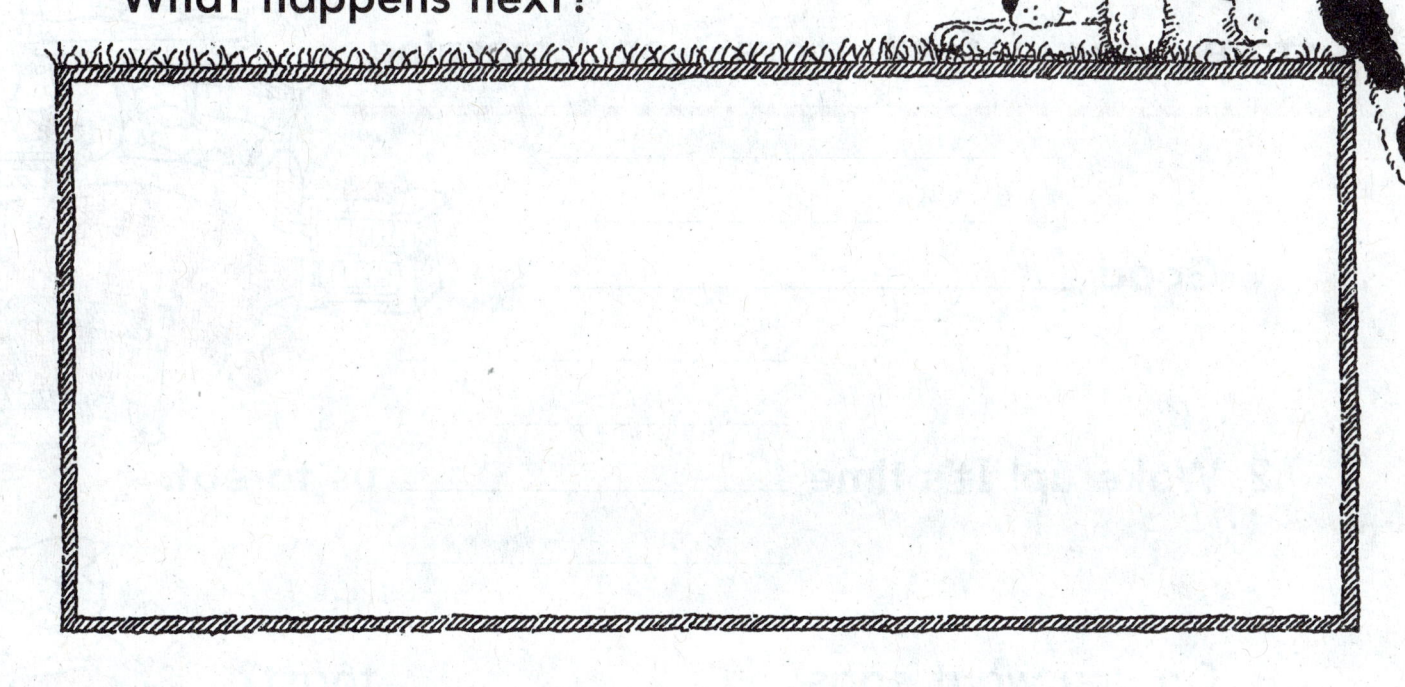

Read the sentences. Write what happens next.

2. A hungry bear catches a fish. Bears love to eat fish. What happens next?

Theme 10: **We Can Do It!**

Name _____

The Vowel + r Sound in *store*

Write a word from the box to complete each sentence.

Word Bank

store   corn   for   more   or   morning

1. Good _____ !

2. Wake up! It's time _____ us to eat.

3. Do you want eggs _____ toast?

4. We need _____ milk and eggs.

5. We also need a can of _____ .

6. We'll go to the _____ later.

Theme 10: **We Can Do It!**

Name _____

Week 1

Vocabulary Math Words

Whole or Half?

Write a word from the box to complete each sentence.

Word Bank

| divide | equal | whole | half | halves |

1. This is a _____ pie.

2. We will _____ the pie.

3. We'll cut it into two _____ parts.

4. Now the pie is in two _____ .

5. Each of us gets one _____ of the pie.

Theme 10: **We Can Do It!** 249

Name _____

Week 1

Grammar Describing What We Hear

Sound Match

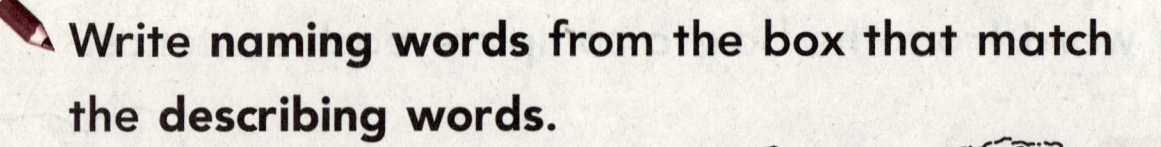

Write **naming words** from the box that match the **describing words**.

Word Bank

bee   car horn   bell   drum   cat

Describing Words   **Naming Words**

1. **clanging, ringing**   _____

2. **loud, beeping**   _____

3. **soft, purring**   _____

4. **buzzing, humming**   _____

5. **tapping, beating**   _____

Theme 10: **We Can Do It!**

Name _____

Week 1

Spelling The Vowel + r Sound in *store*

Spelling Spree

Write the missing letters to complete each Spelling Word. Write the word.

Spelling Words

store
corn
for
more
or
morning

1. f __ __   _____

2. c __ __ n _____

3. m __ __ e _____

Proofread each sentence. Circle each Spelling Word that is wrong, and write it correctly.

4. What a nice moerning.   _____

5. I need two ore three books.   _____

6. I'll look in this stoar.   _____

Theme 10: **We Can Do It!**   251

Name _____

My Book Report

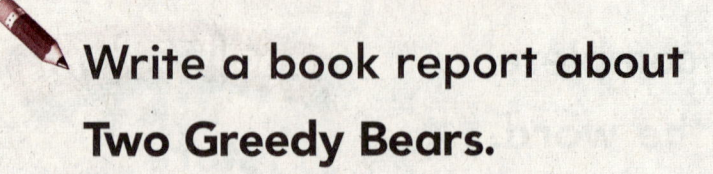

Write a book report about **Two Greedy Bears.**

Title: _____

Author: _____

What is the book about?

_____
_____
_____

What did you like about the book?

_____
_____
_____
_____

Name _____

Reading-Writing Workshop

Revising Your Instructions

Revising Your Instructions

Check the sentences that tell about your writing.

Superstar

☐ I have a good beginning sentence.
☐ My instructions are in 1-2-3 order.
☐ I used time-order words.
☐ I wrote about something I know how to do well and can explain clearly.
☐ My instructions are easy to follow and interesting to read.

Rising Star

☐ I need to put my instructions in 1-2-3 order.
☐ I need to add time-order words.
☐ I need to explain this better.

Theme 10: **We Can Do It!** 253

Name _____

Writing Clear Sentences

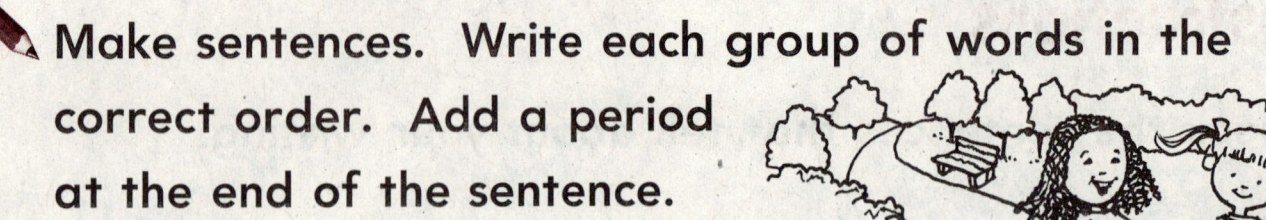

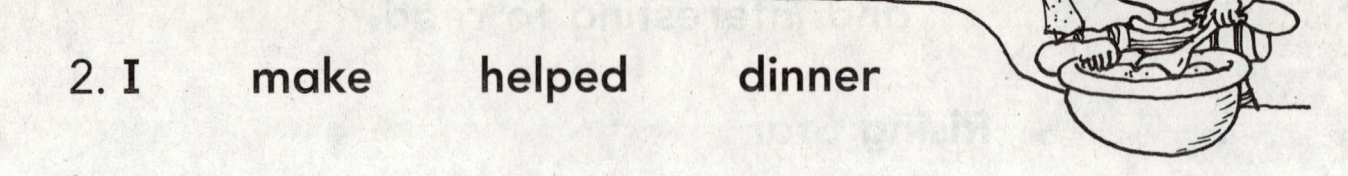

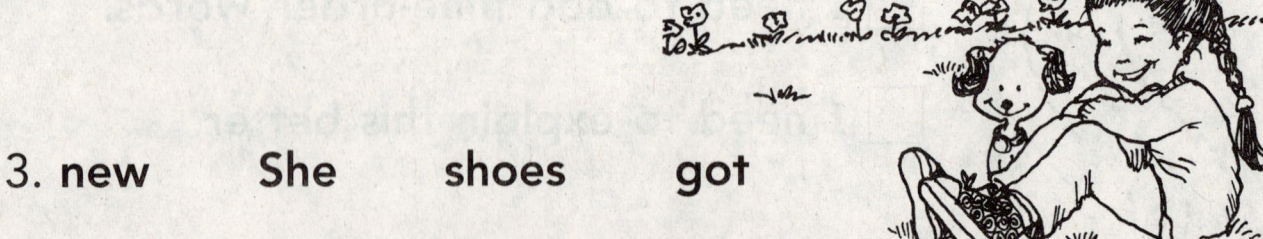

Make sentences. Write each group of words in the correct order. Add a period at the end of the sentence.

1. park   to   We   the   went

_____

_____

2. I   make   helped   dinner

_____

_____

3. new   She   shoes   got

_____

_____

Name _____

Week 2

Phonics *r*-Controlled Vowels: *ar*

A Hard Time

Read the rhyme. Circle the words that have the vowel + r sound as in **car**.

My car will not start!

It needs a new part.

I'd be better off by far
with a horse and a cart!

Write a sentence to answer the question.

Why is the man having a hard time?

_____
_____
_____
_____

Write two words from the rhyme to answer this riddle.

Both have wheels. What are they?

_____   _____

Theme 10: **We Can Do It!**   255

Name _____

Week 2
Phonics *r*-Controlled Vowels: *ar*

Climb Down the Barn

Read the word at the top of the barn.
Read the directions, and write the new words.
The starred one is done for you.

⭐ Take out the last **t** in **tart**.
1. Change the **t** to **c**.
2. Change the **c** to **j**.
3. Change the **j** to **f**.
4. Add **m** to the end.

tart

⭐ t a r

1. ___ ___ ___

2. ___ ___ ___

3. ___ ___ ___

4. ___ ___ ___ ___

Now write a sentence about a **barn** on a **farm**.

_____
_____

256 Theme 10: **We Can Do It!**

Name _____

Week 2

High-Frequency Words

Words to Know

Read each pair of sentences. Circle the sentence that goes with the picture.

The baby will begin to walk soon.
The puppy can already walk.

A bird is flying above the tree.
A boy is leaning against the tree.

Jack has just caught his bus.
Jill must wait one more minute.

Theme 10: **We Can Do It!** 257

Name _____

Week 2

High-Frequency Words

Words to Know

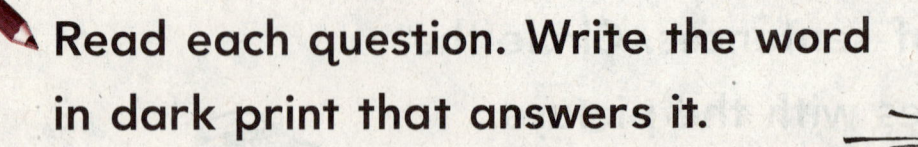

Read each question. Write the word in dark print that answers it.

1. Is Bear **above** the wall or **against** the wall? _____

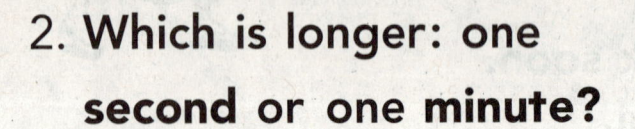

2. Which is longer: one **second** or one **minute**? _____

3. Which word means to start: **begin** or **end**? _____

Circle the picture that answers each question.

4. Who **caught** the ball?

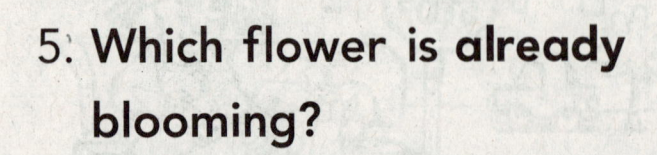

5. Which flower is **already** blooming?

258 Theme 10: **We Can Do It!**

Week 2
Story Vocabulary

Name _____

Carl's Journey

Circle and write the word that completes each sentence.

1. Carl is going on a space _____.

   beacon   journey

2. People _____ to wish him luck.

   appear   whispers

3. "Follow the beacon of light," _____ Andy.

   appears   warns

4. Carl _____ to take pictures.

   promises   beacons

5. This journey is Carl's _____.

   monarch   favorite

Theme 10: **We Can Do It!** 259

Name _____

Week 2

Comprehension Check
Fireflies for Nathan

What Happened Next?

These sentences about Nathan are mixed up. Cut out and paste them in the correct order.

1	2
3	4

| Nathan caught fireflies in the jar. | Nathan went to stay with Nana and Poppy. |
| Nathan took the jar and went to bed. | Nathan waited for it to get dark. |

Theme 10: **We Can Do It!** 261

Name _____

Week 2

Comprehension Sequence of Events

A Bug's Day

Look at the picture story. Write **1**, **2**, or **3** beside each sentence to tell what happens at the **beginning**, **middle**, and **end**.

1 2 3

_____ The bug crawled under a leaf.

_____ The sleepy bug rested in the sun.

_____ Then it started to rain hard.

Write a sentence to tell what the bug did next.

_____
_____
_____
_____
_____
_____

Theme 10: **We Can Do It!** 263

Name _____

Week 2

Spelling The Vowel + r Sound in c*ar*

The Vowel + r Sound in *car*

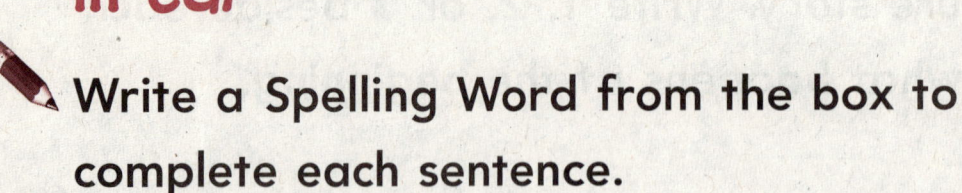

Write a Spelling Word from the box to complete each sentence.

Spelling Words

car
start
arm
far
yard
dark

1. It's a _____ night.

2. Dad just drove off in his _____ .

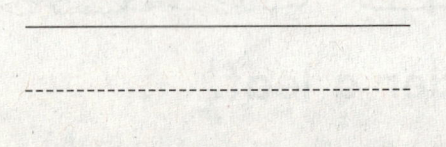

3. He waved good-bye with his _____ .

4. Now he is _____ away.

5. I already miss our house and _____ .

6. I hope I'll _____ to like camp soon!

264 Theme 10: **We Can Do It!**

Week 2

Vocabulary Prefixes *dis-*, *re-*

Name _____

Old Words, New Parts

Write a word from the box to complete one sentence in each pair.

Word Bank

reopen   dislikes   discolored   rebuild

1. This doghouse is too small for our new dog.

   We will have to _____ it.

2. The store is closed. It will _____ at three.

3. Our cat is not happy when it rains.

   He _____ getting wet.

4. There is a leak in the tub.

   It left a _____ spot.

Theme 10: **We Can Do It!** 265

Name _____

Week 2

Grammar More Describing Words

Taste, Smell, Feel

Circle and write the word that tells about what is shown in the picture.

1. This feels _____ .

   fizzy   soft   spicy

2. This tastes _____ .

   creamy   loud   hard

3. This feels _____ .

   shiny   fuzzy   wet

4. This smells _____ .

   smoky   sweet   hard

5. This tastes _____ .

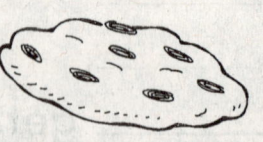

   shiny   small   sweet

6. This smells _____ .

   fresh   fuzzy   cold

Theme 10: **We Can Do It!**

Name _____

Week 2

Spelling The Vowel + *r* Sound in *car*

Spelling Spree

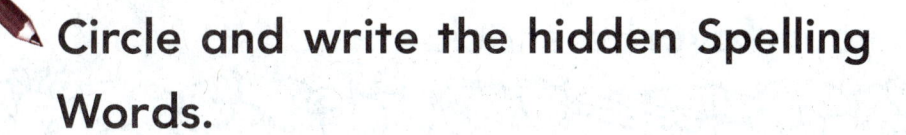

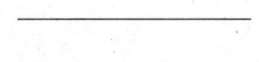

Circle and write the hidden Spelling Words.

Spelling Words

car
start
arm
far
yard
dark

1. mcarls _____

2. abfarl _____

3. clarme _____

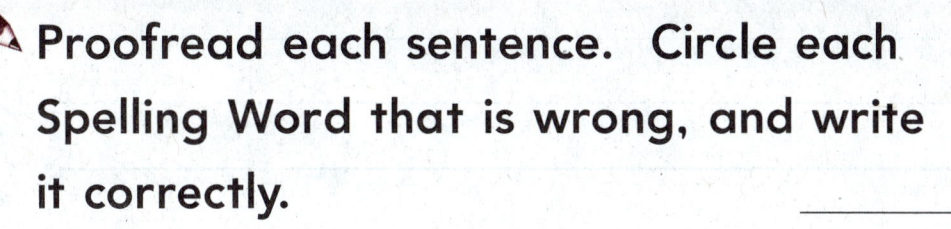

Proofread each sentence. Circle each Spelling Word that is wrong, and write it correctly.

4. I am out in the yerd. _____

5. It is getting durk. _____

6. When do the fireflies sturt? _____

Theme 10: **We Can Do It!** 267

Name _____

Week 2

Writing Writing Clearly with Describing Words

Snack Facts

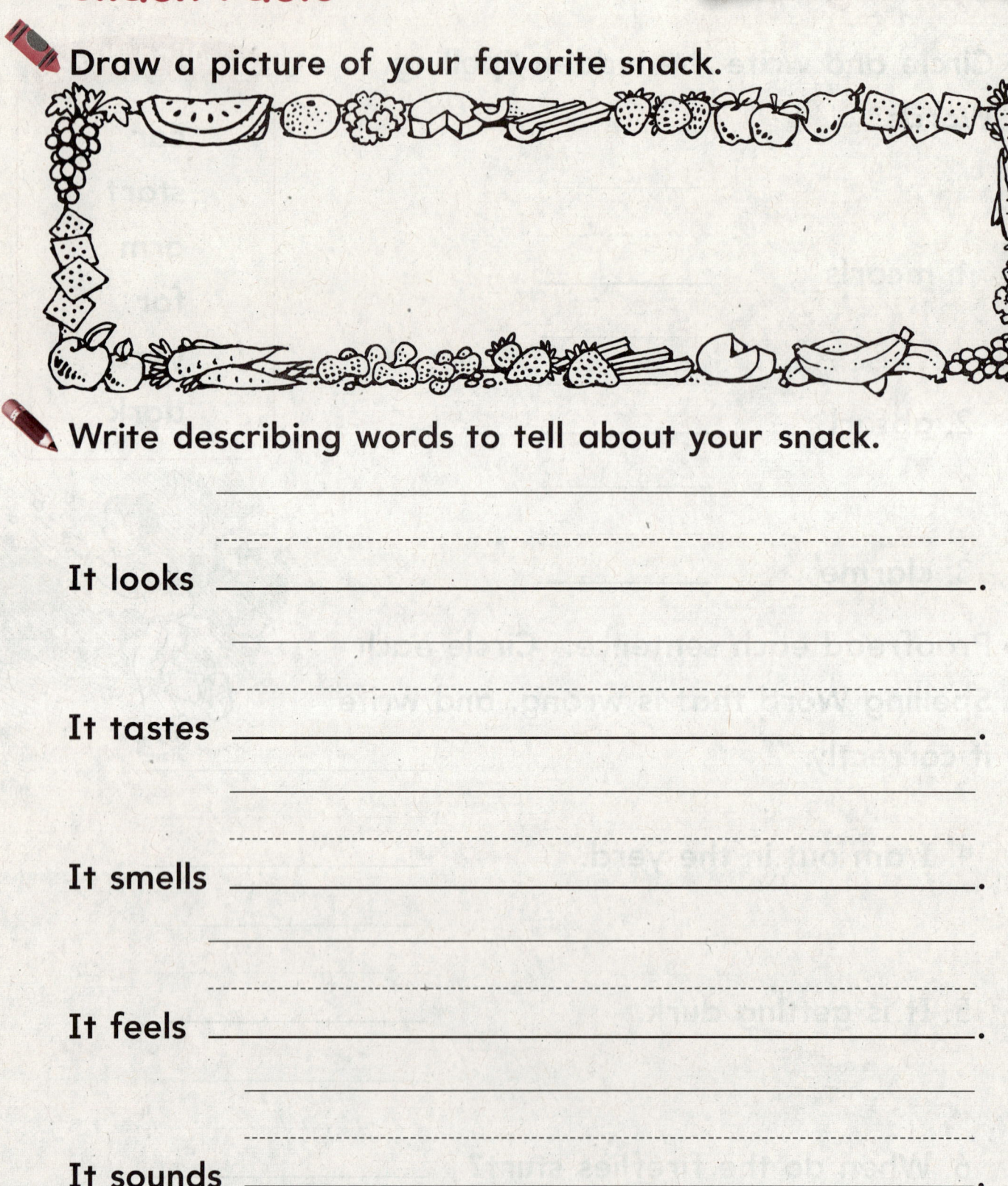

Draw a picture of your favorite snack.

Write describing words to tell about your snack.

It looks _____.

It tastes _____.

It smells _____.

It feels _____.

It sounds _____.

Theme 10: We Can Do It!

Name _____

Week 3

Phonics Base Words and Endings -er, -est

Proud of My Sister

Circle the word that makes sense in each sentence.

1. My sister Gail is _____ than I am.
   older   oldest   old

2. We are the _____ sisters I know.
   close   closer   closest

3. Gail is the _____ runner in our school.
   fasting   fastest   faster

4. She can also run _____ than anyone.
   longer   longing   longest

5. She is the _____ person to beat.
   hardly   harder   hardest

6. I am the _____ sister around!
   proudest   proud   proudly

Theme 10: **We Can Do It!** 269

Name _____

Words to Know

Read the story.

I was able to run to the store today. I had a smart thought. I got you a present. Close one eye at a time.

What do you think the present is? Draw and write your answer.

Week 3

High-Frequency Words

270 Theme 10: **We Can Do It!**

Name _____

Week 3
High-Frequency Words

Words to Know

Finish each sentence with a word from the Word Bank. Write each word in the correct puzzle boxes.

Word Bank

able   eye   present   thought

Across

1. We were ____ to go to the party after all.
2. That ____ is for you.

Down

3. Keep one ____ on the present.
4. Have you ____ about what it might be?

Write a sentence using some words from the box.

_____
_____
_____
_____

Theme 10: **We Can Do It!**   271

Name _____

Week 3
Story Vocabulary

A Present from Ed

Circle and write the word that completes each sentence.

1. I got flowers on my _____ .

   sorry   birthday

2. They were so _____ !

   birthday   beautiful

3. One was a _____ sunflower.

   giant   delighted

4. Some flowers were _____ .

   sorry   smaller

5. My birthday was so nice and _____ .

   pleasant   giant

272 Theme 10: **We Can Do It!**

Name _____

Week 3

Comprehension Check
The Hat

What Was the Cause?

Answer the questions.

1. Why did Frog give Toad a hat?

   It was Toad's _____ .

2. Why was Toad sad for a while?

   The hat _____ .

3. Why was Toad much happier at the end of the story?

   The hat _____ .

Theme 10: **We Can Do It!**   273

Name _____

Week 3

Comprehension Cause and Effect

Mr. Bear's Bad Morning

Read the story. Complete each sentence with a group of words from the box.

Mr. Bear woke up late. He had to rush out without eating. He missed the bus and had to walk to work. On the way, it started to rain. He had not worn his raincoat. He got very wet!

---
got wet   missed the bus   was hungry
---

1. Mr. Bear _____ because he rushed out without eating.

2. Mr. Bear walked to work because he _____.

3. Mr. Bear _____ because he didn't have his raincoat.

274   Theme 10: **We Can Do It!**

Week 3

Spelling Adding *-er* and *-est* to Words

Name _____

Adding *er* and *est* to Words

Spelling Words

- newer
- warmest
- highest
- faster
- deepest
- richer

Write a Spelling Word from the box to complete each sentence.

1. Today is the _____ day of the summer.

2. This pool is _____ than the old one in town.

3. Otter swam _____ than anyone else.

4. Now Otter is at the _____ spot.

5. Otter dove into the _____ water.

6. Otter feels _____ than a king!

Theme 10: **We Can Do It!** 275

Week 3

Vocabulary Suffix -*ly*

Name _____

How Do They Do It?

Look at the pictures. Write a word from the box to complete each sentence.

Word Bank

| tightly | kindly | quickly | loudly | slowly |

1. Snail crawls _____.

2. Rabbit runs _____.

3. Frog croaks _____.

4. Cat smiles _____.

5. Dog holds on _____.

276   Theme 10: **We Can Do It!**

Name _____

Week 3

Grammar Adding -er and -est

Puzzle Fun

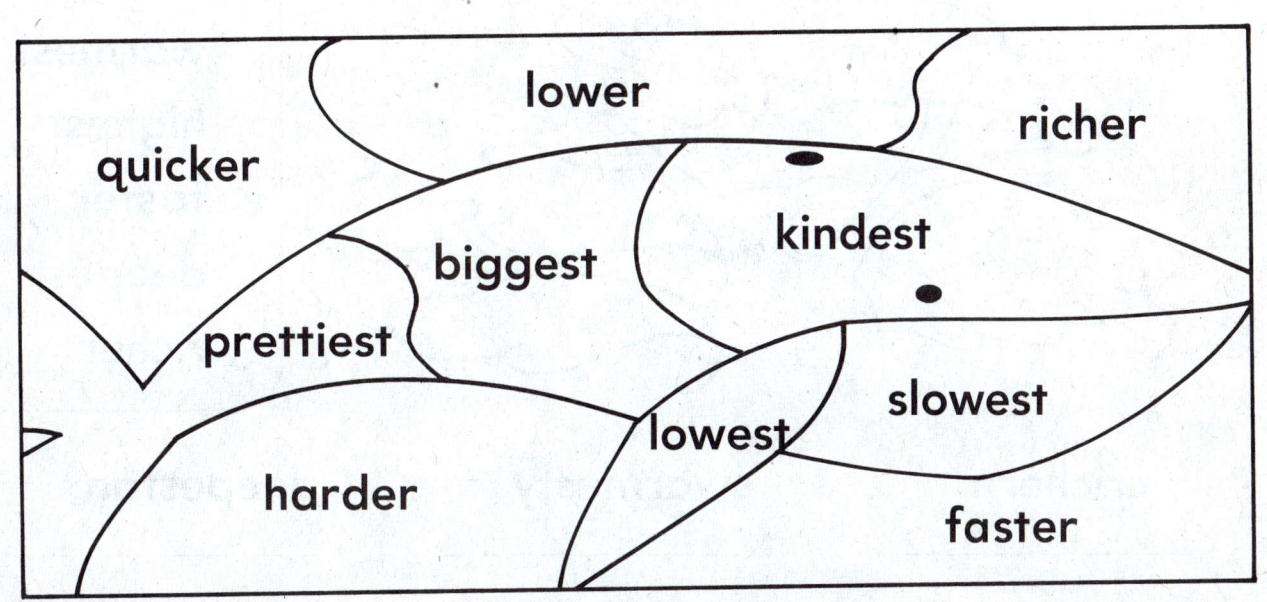

Color blue the puzzle parts that have words comparing more than two people or things.

quicker, lower, richer, biggest, kindest, prettiest, lowest, slowest, harder, faster

Circle and write the word that completes each sentence.

1. The blue whale is the _____ of all animals today.

    bigger   biggest

2. It is _____ than any other animal.

    bigger   biggest

Theme 10: **We Can Do It!** 277

Week 3

Spelling Adding -er and -est

Name _____

Spelling Spree

Circle and write the hidden Spelling Words.

Spelling Words

newer
warmest
highest
faster
deepest
richer

crichern   swarmesty   deepestan

1. _____   2. _____   3. _____

Proofread each sentence. Circle each Spelling Word that is wrong, and write it correctly.

4. Birds are in the hies tree. _____

5. They want a newr nest. _____

6. They work fastur than ever. _____

278 Theme 10: **We Can Do It!**

Name _____

Week 3
Writing Thank-You Note

Thanks!

Write a thank-you note.

_____

Dear _____,

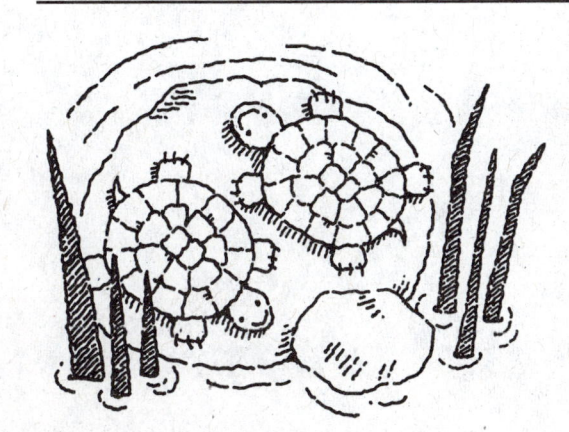

_____
_____
_____
_____
_____
_____
_____

Your friend,

_____
_____

Theme 10: **We Can Do It!** 279

We Can Do It!

Taking Tests

Name _____

Writing a Personal Narrative

Use what you have learned about taking tests. First, make a chart to help you plan. Next, write your narrative. Then see how you can make your answer better.

In **Two Greedy Bears**, the bear cubs learn that arguing doesn't always solve their problems. Write about a time when you solved a problem without arguing.

Name _____

We Can Do It!

Taking Tests

Writing a Personal Narrative

continued

✏ Read your personal narrative. Check off each box that tells about your answer.

☐ The beginning tells what my narrative is about.

☐ My narrative has the words **I** and **me**.

☐ My narrative has details that help the reader picture what happened.

☐ The ending tells how I felt.

✏ If you did not check a box, you can make your answer better. Make your changes here.

_____
_____
_____
_____
_____
_____

282 Theme 10: **We Can Do It!**

Name _____

**We Can Do It!:
Theme 10 Wrap-Up**

Spelling Review

Spelling Review

Write the Spelling Words that have the same vowel + r sounds you hear in the two words below.

Spelling Words

corn
newer
faster
more
warmest
dark

for   car

1. _____   3. _____

2. _____

Add an ending to each word to make a Spelling Word from the box. Write the Spelling Word.

4. warm _____

5. new _____

6. fast _____

Theme 10: **We Can Do It!**   283

Name _____

**We Can Do It!:
Theme 10 Wrap-Up**
Spelling Review

Spelling Spree

✏️ Write the Spelling Word that goes with the words in each group.

Spelling Words

more
arm
morning
yard
highest
faster

1. tallest, longest, _____

2. bigger, stronger, _____

3. leg, head, _____

✏️ Proofread each sentence. Circle each Spelling Word that is wrong, and write it correctly.

4. I need a person to mow my yawrd.

5. You can start in the moorning.

6. Find out mor at 344 Garden Lane.

284   Theme 10: **We Can Do It!**

My Handbook

Contents

Alphafriends — 288

Phonics/Decoding Strategy — 290

Reading Strategies — 291

Writing the Alphabet — 292

Spelling
    How to Study a Word — 300
    Special Words for Writing — 301
    Take-Home Word Lists — 303

Proofreading Checklist — 327

Proofreading Marks — 327

Alphafriends

a — Andy Apple

b — Benny Bear

c — Callie Cat

d — Dudley Duck

e — Edna Elephant

f — Fifi Fish

g — Gertie Goose

h — Hattie Horse

i — Iggy Iguana

j — Jumping Jill

k — Keely Kangaroo

l — Larry Lion

m — Mimi Mouse

Alphafriends

Nyle Noodle

Ozzie Octopus

Pippa Pig

Queenie Queen

Reggie Rooster

Sammy Seal

Tiggy Tiger

Umbie Umbrella

Vinny Volcano

Willy Worm

Mr. X-Ray

Yetta Yo-Yo

Zelda Zebra

My Handbook 289

Phonics Decoding Strategy

1. Look at the letters from left to right.

2. Think about the sounds for the letters, and look for word parts you know.

3. Blend the sounds to read the word.

4. Ask yourself: **Is it a word I know? Does it make sense in what I am reading?**

5. If not, ask yourself: **What else can I try?**

Reading Strategies

Predict/Infer
▶ Think about the title, the illustrations, and what you have read so far.
▶ Tell what you think will happen next or what you will learn.

Question
▶ Ask yourself questions as you read.

Monitor/Clarify
▶ Ask yourself if what you are reading makes sense.
▶ If you don't understand something, reread, read ahead, or use the illustrations.

Summarize
▶ Think about the main ideas or the important parts of the story.
▶ Tell the important things in your own words.

Evaluate
▶ Ask yourself: Do I like what I have read? Am I learning what I wanted to know?

Writing the Alphabet

✏️ **Trace and write the letters.**

Aa Aa

Bb Bb

Cc Cc

Dd Dd

Ee Ee

Ff Ff

Gg Gg

Writing the Alphabet

Trace and write the letters.

Hh Hh

Ii Ii

Jj Jj

Kk Kk

Ll Ll

Mm Mm

My Handbook 293

Writing the Alphabet

✏️ Trace and write the letters.

Nn Nn

Oo Oo

Pp Pp

Qq Qq

Rr Rr

Ss Ss

Tt Tt

My Handbook

Writing the Alphabet

✏️ **Trace and write the letters.**

Uu Uu

Vv Vv

Ww Ww

Xx Xx

Yy Yy

Zz Zz

Writing the Alphabet

✏️ **Trace and write the letters.**

Aa Aa

Bb Bb

Cc Cc

Dd Dd

Ee Ee

Ff Ff

Gg Gg

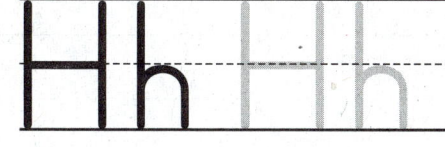

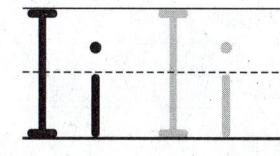

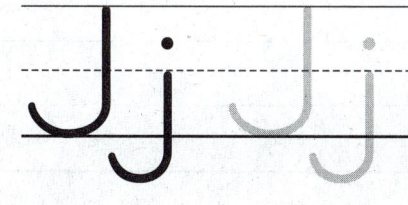

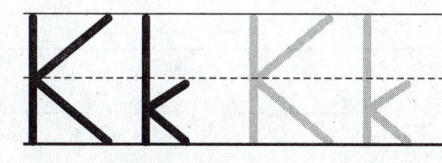

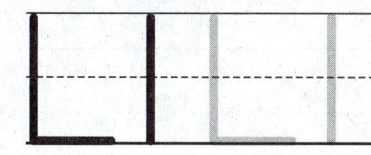

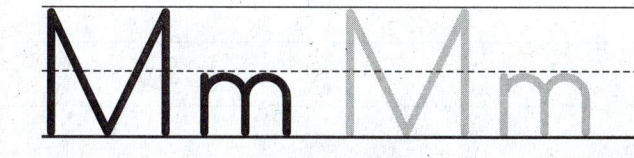

Writing the Alphabet

Trace and write the letters.

Hh Hh

Ii Ii

Jj Jj

Kk Kk

Ll Ll

Mm Mm

My Handbook

Writing the Alphabet

✏️ **Trace and write the letters.**

Nn Nn

Oo Oo

Pp Pp

Qq Qq

Rr Rr

Ss Ss

Tt Tt

298 My Handbook

Writing the Alphabet

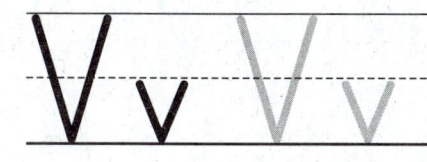

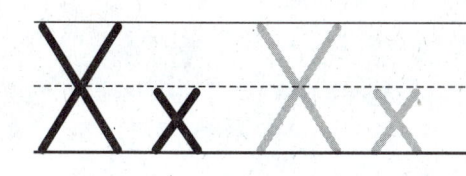

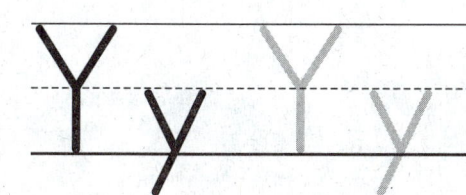

Trace and write the letters.

Uu Uu

Vv Vv

Ww Ww

Xx Xx

Yy Yy

Zz Zz

Spelling

How to Study a Word

1. **LOOK** at the word.

2. **SAY** the word.

3. **THINK** about the word.

4. **WRITE** the word.

5. **CHECK** the spelling.

Special Words for Writing

A
a
about
again
all
always
and
any
around
as

B
back
because
before

C
cannot
come
coming
could

D
do
down

F
for
friend
from

G
getting
goes
going

H
has
have
her
here
his
house
how

I
I
if
into
is

L
little

M
many
more

N
never
new
now

Special Words for Writing

O
of
one
or
other
our
out
over

P
people

R
right

S
said
some

T
than
the
their
there
they
thing
to
tried
two

V
very

W
want
was
were
what
when
where
who
would

Y
you
your

Take-Home Word List

Me on the Map

The Long *a* Sound

make

came

take

Spelling Words

1. make
2. came
3. take
4. name
5. gave
6. game

Challenge Words

1. place
2. skate

My Study List
Add your own spelling words on the back. ➡

303

Take-Home Word List

Moving Day

Words Spelled with *sh* or *ch*

she   chin

fish   much

Spelling Words

1. she
2. chin
3. fish
4. shell
5. much
6. chop

Challenge Words

1. shoe
2. chair

My Study List
Add your own spelling words on the back. ➡

303

Take-Home Word List

Name _____

My Study List

1. _____
2. _____
3. _____
4. _____
5. _____
6. _____

Take-Home Word List

Name _____

My Study List

1. _____
2. _____
3. _____
4. _____
5. _____
6. _____

Take-Home Word List

Home Sweet Home
Spelling Review

Spelling Words
1. shell
2. make
3. like
4. fish
5. gave
6. kite
7. ride
8. chop
9. name
10. much

See the back for Challenge Words.

My Study List
Add your own spelling words on the back. →

Take-Home Word List

The Kite

The Long *i* Sound
like
five

Spelling Words
1. like
2. five
3. ride
4. nine
5. time
6. kite

Challenge Words
1. prize
2. smile

My Study List
Add your own spelling words on the back. →

Take-Home Word List

Name _____

My Study List

1. _____
2. _____
3. _____
4. _____
5. _____
6. _____

Take-Home Word List

Name _____

My Study List

1. _____
2. _____
3. _____
4. _____
5. _____
6. _____

Challenge Words

1. chair
2. place
3. prize

Take-Home Word List

EEK! There's a Mouse in the House

The Long e Sound

me
see
mean

Spelling Words

1. me
2. see
3. mean
4. feet
5. eat
6. he

Challenge Words

1. maybe
2. sheep

My Study List
Add your own spelling words on the back. ➡

Take-Home Word List

The Sleeping Pig

The Long o Sound

go
bone
nose

Spelling Words

1. go
2. bone
3. so
4. nose
5. home
6. no

Challenge Words

1. also
2. woke

My Study List
Add your own spelling words on the back. ➡

Take-Home Word List

Name _____

My Study List

1. _____
2. _____
3. _____
4. _____
5. _____
6. _____

Take-Home Word List

Name _____

My Study List

1. _____
2. _____
3. _____
4. _____
5. _____
6. _____

Take-Home Word List

Animal Adventures Spelling Review

Spelling Words

1. go
2. me
3. day
4. feet
5. nose
6. eat
7. play
8. mean
9. home
10. stay

See the back for Challenge Words.

My Study List Add your own spelling words on the back.

Take-Home Word List

Red-Eyed Tree Frog

The Long *a* Sound Spelled *ay*

day   say
play

Spelling Words

1. day
2. say
3. play
4. may
5. way
6. stay

Challenge Words

1. away
2. holiday

My Study List Add your own spelling words on the back.

Take-Home Word List

Name _____

📝 My Study List

1. _____
2. _____
3. _____
4. _____
5. _____
6. _____

Take-Home Word List

Name _____

📝 My Study List

1. _____
2. _____
3. _____
4. _____
5. _____
6. _____

Challenge Words

1. woke
2. sheep
3. away

Take-Home Word List

Lost!

The Vowel Sound in *book*

look   foot
good

Spelling Words
1. look
2. book
3. took
4. good
5. foot
6. cook

Challenge Words
1. hoof
2. crook

My Study List
Add your own spelling words on the back.

Take-Home Word List

That Toad Is Mine!

More Long *o* Spellings

boat   slow
coat   grow

Spelling Words
1. boat
2. slow
3. coat
4. grow
5. show
6. toad

Challenge Words
1. coast
2. know

My Study List
Add your own spelling words on the back.

Take-Home Word List

Name _____

📝 **My Study List**

_____

1. _____

2. _____

3. _____

4. _____

5. _____

6. _____

312

Take-Home Word List

Name _____

📝 **My Study List**

_____

1. _____

2. _____

3. _____

4. _____

5. _____

6. _____

312

Take-Home Word List

We Can Work It Out
Spelling Review

Spelling Words

1. toad
2. look
3. good
4. grow
5. book
6. too
7. zoo
8. show
9. moon
10. coat

See the back for Challenge Words.

My Study List
Add your own spelling words on the back. ➡

Take-Home Word List

If You Give a Pig a Pancake

The Vowel Sound in *moon*

zoo   soon
food

Spelling Words

1. zoo
2. food
3. too
4. moon
5. soon
6. room

Challenge Words

1. moose
2. balloon

My Study List
Add your own spelling words on the back. ➡

Take-Home Word List

Name _____

📝 My Study List

1. _____
2. _____
3. _____
4. _____
5. _____
6. _____

314

Take-Home Word List

Name _____

📝 My Study List

1. _____
2. _____
3. _____
4. _____
5. _____
6. _____

Challenge Words

1. know
2. hoof
3. moose

314

Take-Home Word List

Butterfly

The Vowel Sound in *cow*

house   down
out   now

Spelling Words

1. cow
2. house
3. out
4. down
5. now
6. found

Challenge Words

1. pouch
2. crowded

My Study List
Add your own spelling words on the back.

Take-Home Word List

The Forest

Adding *s* to Naming Words

cups
trees

Spelling Words

1. cup
2. cups
3. frog
4. frogs
5. tree
6. trees

Challenge Words

1. gloves
2. birds

My Study List
Add your own spelling words on the back.

Take-Home Word List

Name _____

My Study List

1. _____
2. _____
3. _____
4. _____
5. _____
6. _____

Take-Home Word List

Name _____

My Study List

1. _____
2. _____
3. _____
4. _____
5. _____
6. _____

Take-Home Word List

Our Earth
Spelling Review

Spelling Words

1. frog
2. frogs
3. out
4. sleeping
5. now
6. tree
7. trees
8. filled
9. checking
10. found

See the back for Challenge Words.

My Study List
Add your own spelling words on the back.

Take-Home Word List

Johnny Appleseed

Words That End with *ed* or *ing*

land**ed**   check**ing**
miss**ed**   tell**ing**

Spelling Words

1. landed
2. checking
3. telling
4. missed
5. filled
6. sleeping

Challenge Words

1. bluffing
2. planted

My Study List
Add your own spelling words on the back.

Take-Home Word List

Name _____

My Study List

1. _____
2. _____
3. _____
4. _____
5. _____
6. _____

318

Take-Home Word List

Name _____

My Study List

1. _____
2. _____
3. _____
4. _____
5. _____
6. _____

Challenge Words

1. birds
2. pouch
3. planted

318

Take-Home Word List

The New Friend

Adding *es* to Naming Words

dishes   boxes
dresses   beaches

Spelling Words

1. dishes
2. dresses
3. boxes
4. beaches
5. wishes
6. kisses

Challenge Words

1. classes
2. brushes

My Study List Add your own spelling words on the back.

Take-Home Word List

When I Am Old with You

The Long *i* Sound Spelled *y*

by   fly
try

Spelling Words

1. by
2. my
3. fly
4. try
5. cry
6. why

Challenge Words

1. pry
2. multiply

My Study List Add your own spelling words on the back.

Take-Home Word List

Name _____

My Study List

1. _____
2. _____
3. _____
4. _____
5. _____
6. _____

Take-Home Word List

Name _____

My Study List

1. _____
2. _____
3. _____
4. _____
5. _____
6. _____

Take-Home Word List

Special Friends Spelling Review

Spelling Words

1. cry
2. boxes
3. boy
4. try
5. wishes
6. dresses
7. point
8. fly
9. beaches
10. coin

See the back for Challenge Words.

My Study List
Add your own spelling words on the back.

Take-Home Word List

The Surprise Family

The Vowel Sound in *coin*

soil   boy
point

Spelling Words

1. coin
2. soil
3. boy
4. oil
5. toy
6. point

Challenge Words

1. moist
2. destroy

My Study List
Add your own spelling words on the back.

Take-Home Word List

Name _____

My Study List

1. _____
2. _____
3. _____
4. _____
5. _____
6. _____

Take-Home Word List

Name _____

My Study List

1. _____
2. _____
3. _____
4. _____
5. _____
6. _____

Challenge Words

1. multiply
2. brushes
3. moist

Take-Home Word List

Fireflies for Nathan

The Vowel + r Sound in *car*

far   start
arm

Spelling Words

1. car
2. start
3. arm
4. far
5. yard
6. dark

Challenge Words

1. large
2. jar

My Study List
Add your own spelling words on the back.

Take-Home Word List

Two Greedy Bears

The Vowel + r Sound in *store*

corn   more
for

Spelling Words

1. store
2. corn
3. for
4. more
5. or
6. morning

Challenge Words

1. afford
2. before

My Study List
Add your own spelling words on the back.

Take-Home Word List

Name _____

My Study List

1. _____
2. _____
3. _____
4. _____
5. _____
6. _____

Take-Home Word List

Name _____

My Study List

1. _____
2. _____
3. _____
4. _____
5. _____
6. _____

Take-Home Word List

We Can Do It!
Spelling Review

Spelling Words

1. more
2. newer
3. dark
4. warmest
5. morning
6. highest
7. yard
8. corn
9. faster
10. arm

See the back for Challenge Words.

My Study List
Add your own spelling words on the back.

Take-Home Word List

The Hat

Adding *er* or *est* to Words

newer   warmest
faster   highest

Spelling Words

1. newer
2. warmest
3. highest
4. faster
5. deepest
6. richer

Challenge Words

1. smaller
2. kindest

My Study List
Add your own spelling words on the back.

Take-Home Word List

Name _____

My Study List

1. _____
2. _____
3. _____
4. _____
5. _____
6. _____

Take-Home Word List

Name _____

My Study List

1. _____
2. _____
3. _____
4. _____
5. _____
6. _____

Challenge Words

1. afford
2. jar
3. smaller

Proofreading Checklist

Answer these questions when you check your writing.

☐ Did I begin each sentence with a capital letter?

☐ Did I use the right mark at the end of each sentence? (. ?)

☐ Did I spell each word correctly?

Proofreading Marks		
∧	Add	My aunt came ∧visit. (to)
—	Take out	We ~~were~~ sang songs.

My Handbook

My Notes

A	A	A	B	B	C	C	D	D
E	E	E	F	F	G	G	H	H
I	I	I	J	J	K	K	L	L	M
M	N	N	O	O	P	P	Q	Q
R	R	S	S	T	T	U	U	V
V	W	W	X	X	Y	Y	Z	Z

You can add punctuation marks or other letters to the blanks.

Letter Tray

Letter Tray

| c | a | t |

fold

fold

fold

d	d	c	c	b	b	a	a	a
h	h	g	g	f	f	e	e	e
m	l	l	k	k	j	j	i	i
q	q	p	p	o	o	n	n	m
v	u	u	t	t	s	s	r	r
z	z	y	y	x	x	w	w	v

fold

fold

fold

Theme 5, Week 3	Theme 5, Week 2	Theme 5, Week 1
give	could	grow
good	house	light
her	how	long
little	over	more
try	own	other
was	so	right
fly	world	room
our		these
		small

You can add your own words for sentence building.

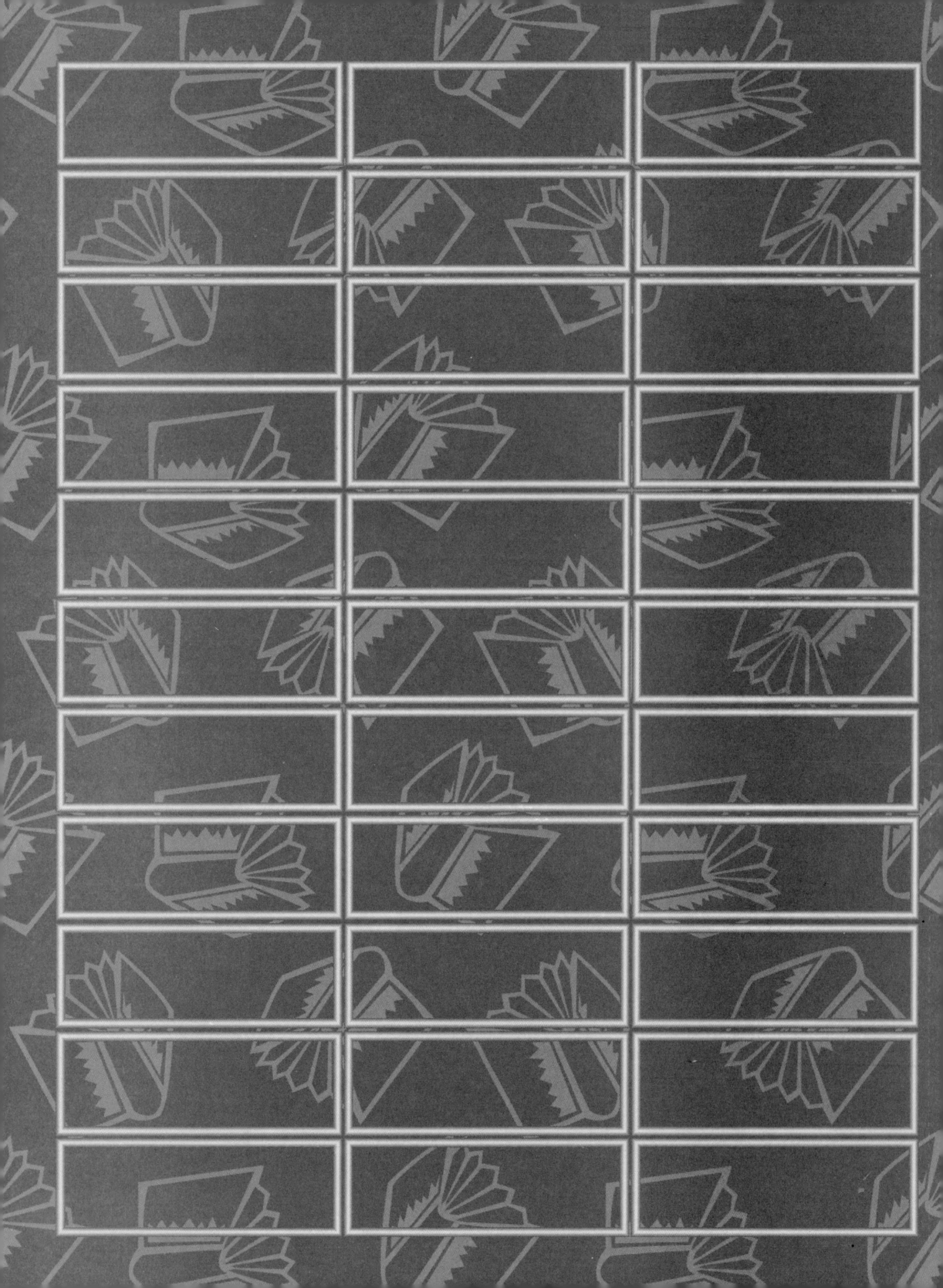

Theme 6, Week 3	Theme 6, Week 2	Theme 6, Week 1
been	cow	morning
far	table	found
forest	now	shout
goes	door	by
hungry	there	out
soon	through	show
evening	horse	climb
near	wall	

You can add your own words for sentence building.

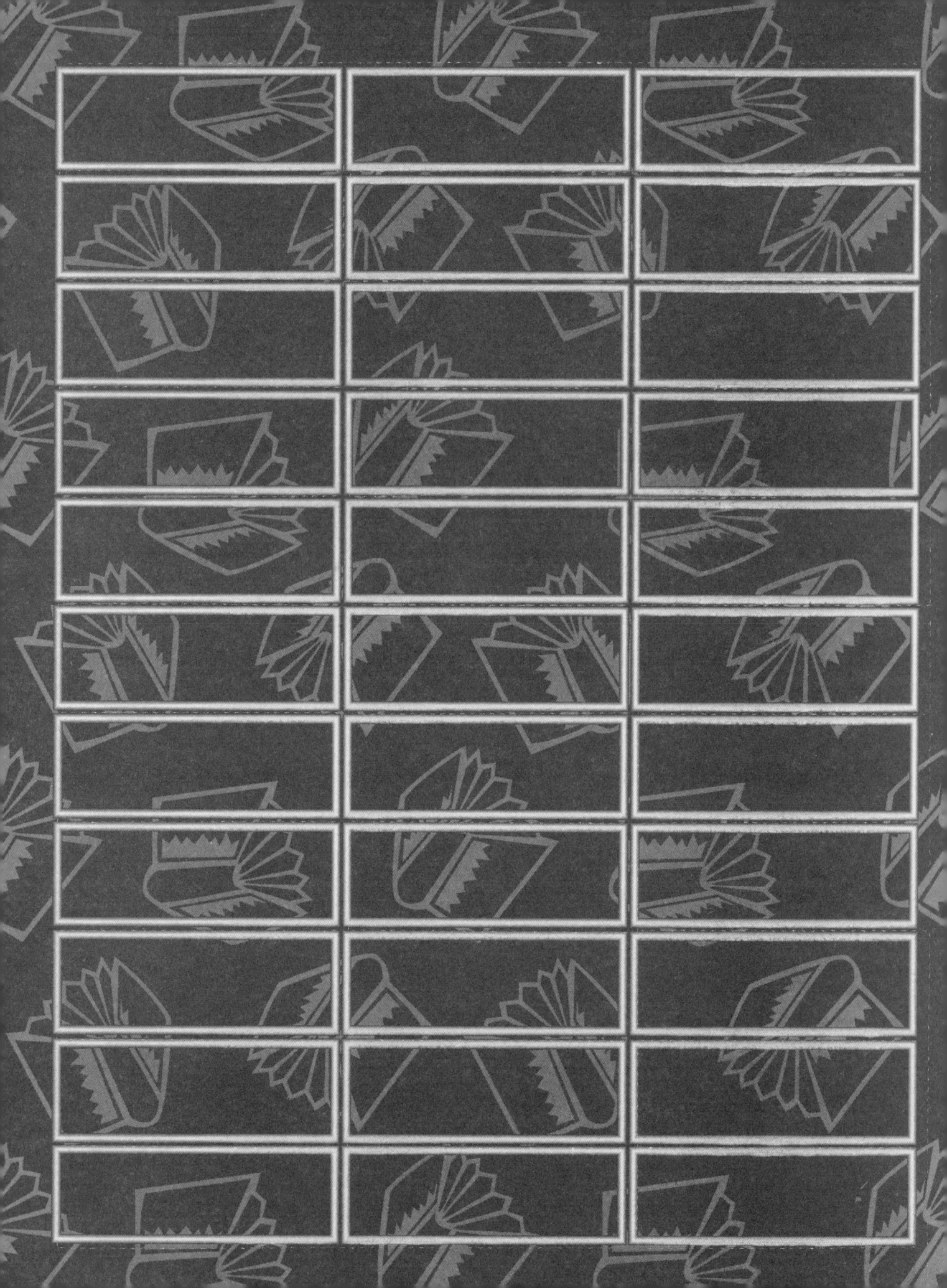

Theme 7, Week 3	Theme 7, Week 2	Theme 7, Week 1
old	afraid	again
piece	any	both
shoe	bear	gone
start	follow	or
under	most	want
very	tall	turn
wear	water	hard
build	idea	

You can add your own words for sentence building.

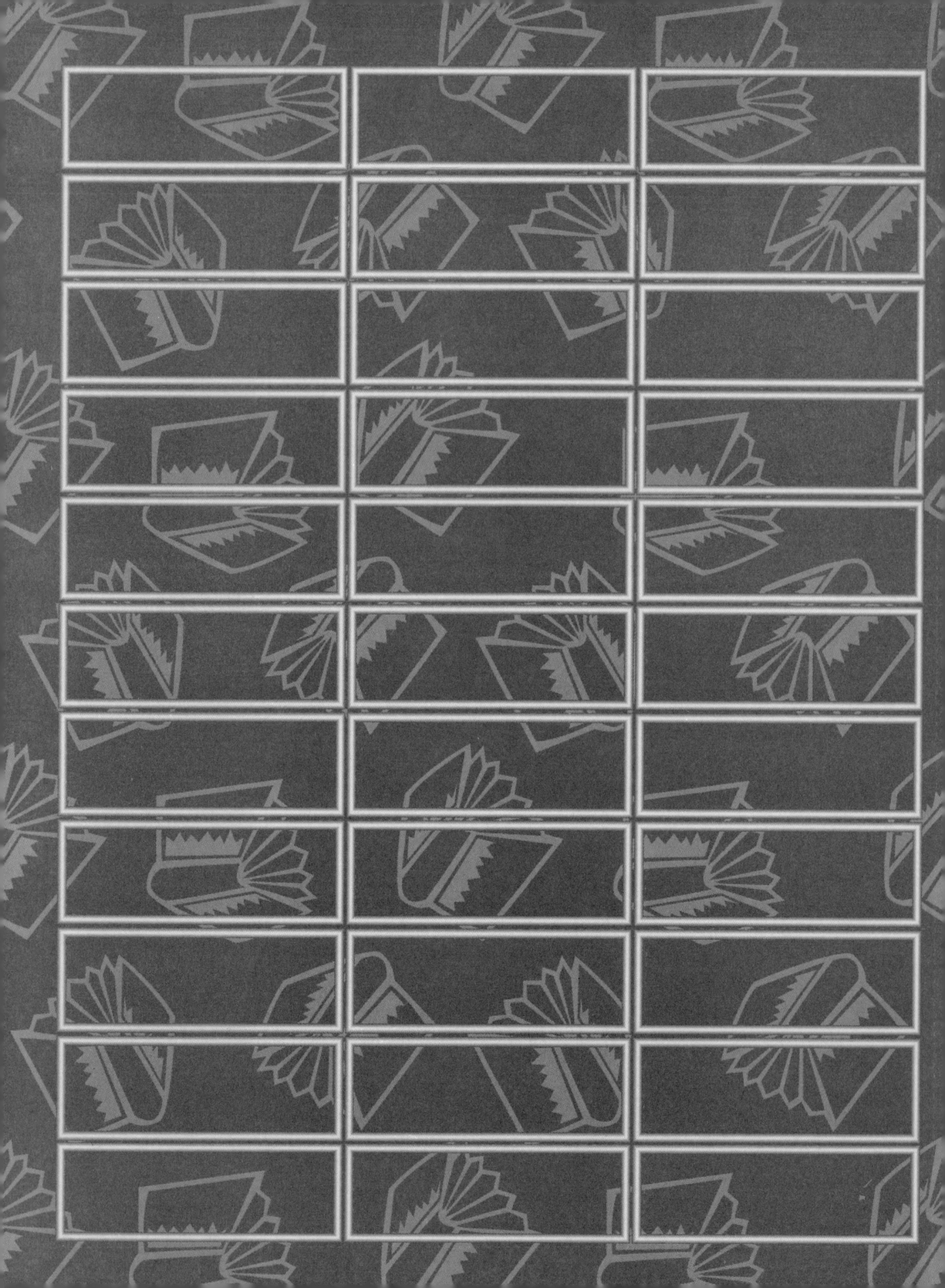

Theme 8, Week 3	Theme 8, Week 2	Theme 8, Week 1
carry	always	about
kind	eight	because
put	arms	draw
saw	seven	happy
butter	warm	teacher
were	ready	part
work	body	tiny
person		

You can add your own words for sentence building.

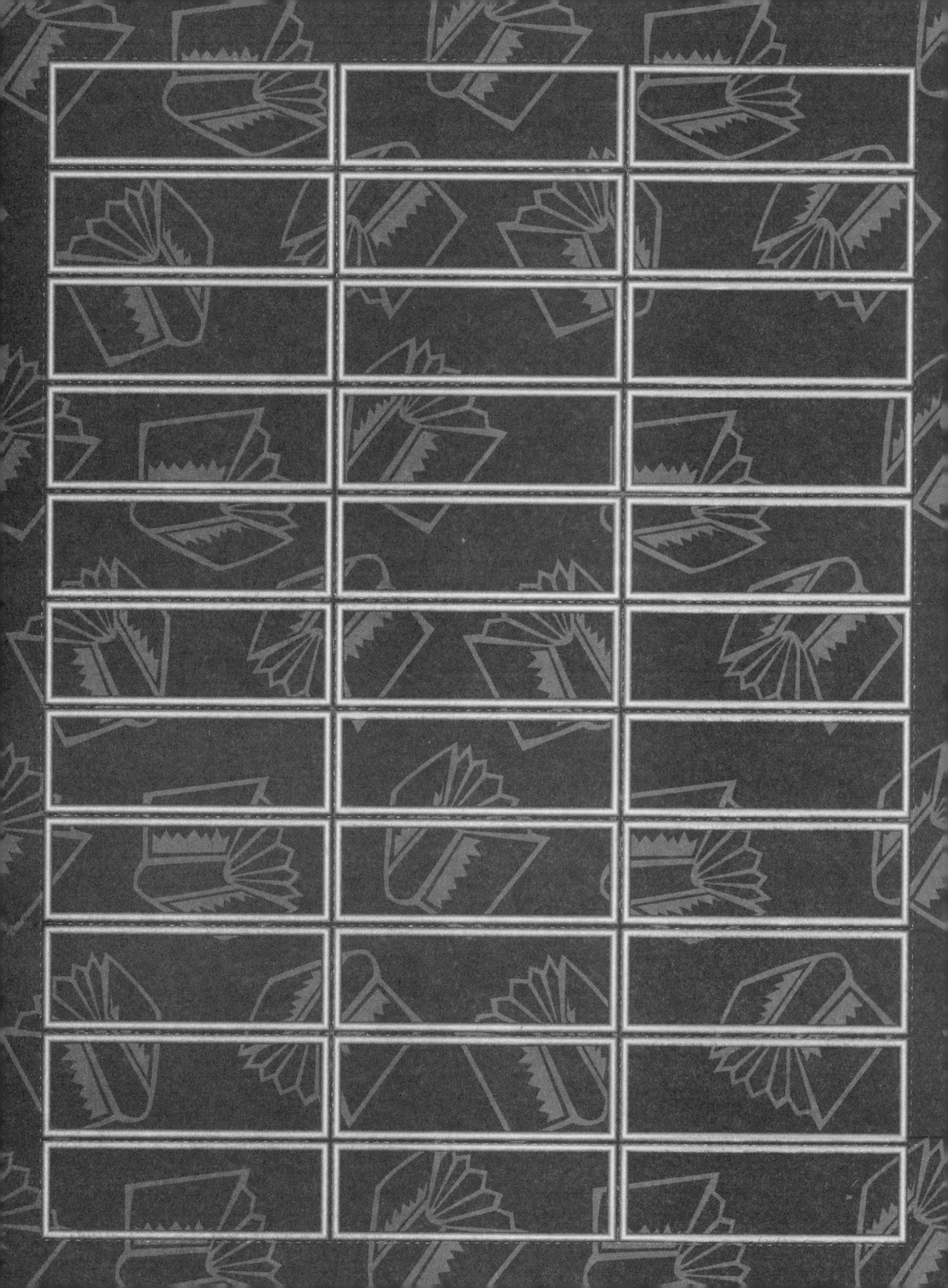

Theme 9, Week 3	Theme 9, Week 2	Theme 9, Week 1
only	after	around
together	before	dance
watched	buy	else
baby	pretty	open
edge	school	talk
enough	done	ever
garden	off	though
sharp	wash	ocean

You can add your own words for sentence building.

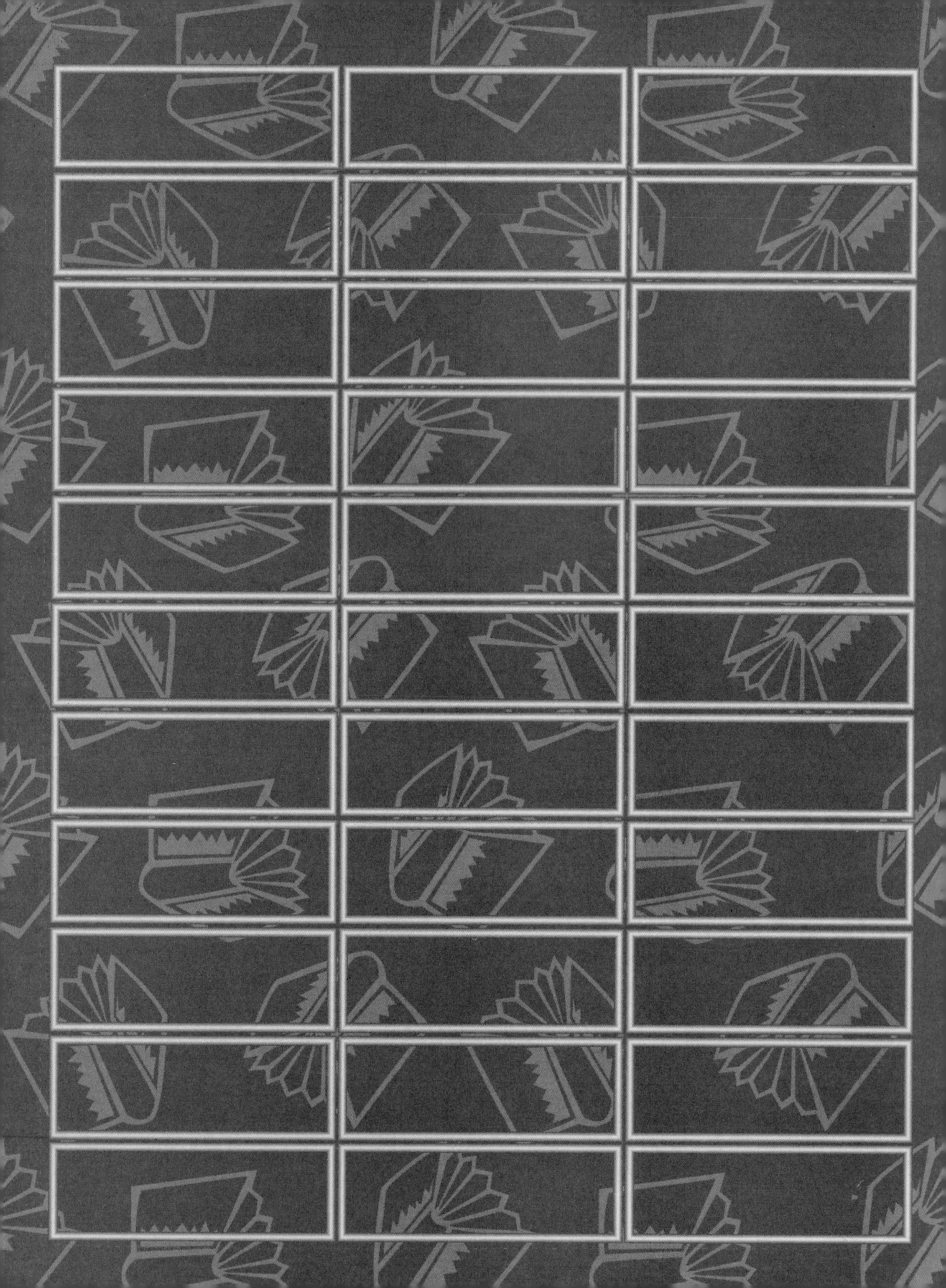

Theme 10, Week 3	Theme 10, Week 2	Theme 10, Week 1
able	above	began
eye	against	laugh
present	already	sure
thoughts	caught	head
	begin	divide
	minute	second
		break

You can add your own words for sentence building.

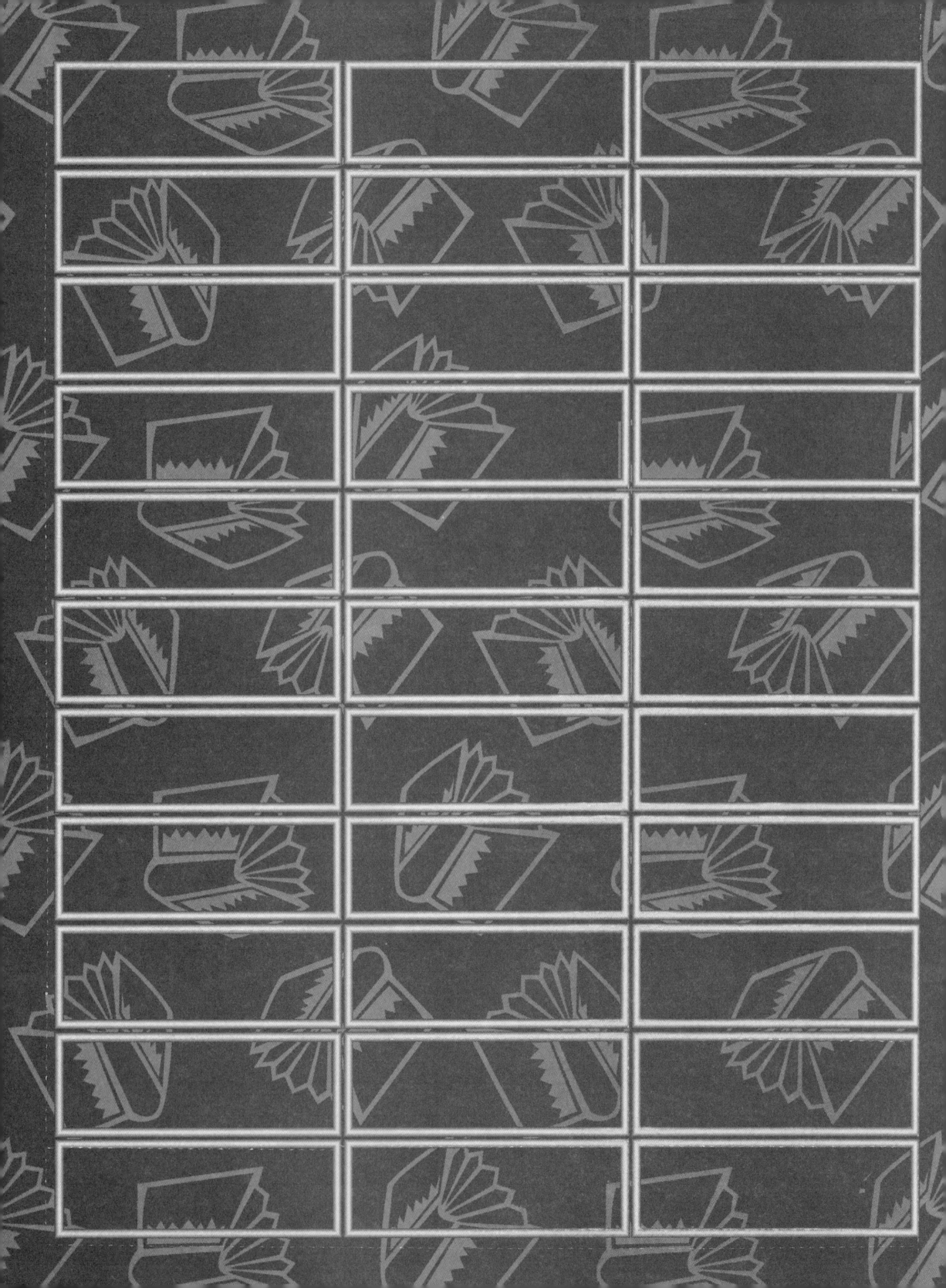